T0049876

CONFESS YOUR SINS

JOHN STOTT

CONFESS YOUR SINS

The Way of Reconciliation

WILLIAM B. EERDMANS PUBLISHING COMPANY

GRAND RAPIDS, MICHIGAN

Wm. B. Eerdmans Publishing Co.
2140 Oak Industrial Drive NE, Grand Rapids, Michigan 49505
www.eerdmans.com

Originally published in the U.K. by Hodder and Stoughton in the Christian
Foundation Series under the title *Confess Your Sins* © 1964, (ASIN: B000oCM2WX).
U.S. edition originally published by Westminster Press, Philadelphia ©1965.
This edition published 2017 by permission of
The Literary Executors of John R. W. Stott.
Printed in the United States of America

26 25 24 23 22 21 20 19 18 17   1 2 3 4 5 6 7 8 9 10

ISBN 978-0-8028-7509-9

Library of Congress Cataloging-in-Publication Data

Names: Stott, John R. W., author.
Title: Confess your sins : the way of reconciliation / John Stott.
Description: Grand Rapids, Michigan : William B. Eerdmans Publishing Company,
   [2017] | Originally published: Philadelphia : Westminster Press, [1965, c1964]. |
   Includes bibliographical references and index.
Identifiers: LCCN 2017006475 | ISBN 9780802875099 (pbk. : alk. paper)
Subjects: LCSH: Confession—Anglican Communion.
Classification: LCC BX5149.C6 S7 2017 | DDC 264/.030862—dc23
   LC record available at https://lccn.loc.gov/2017006475

Contents

Foreword by Ray C. Ortlund Jr.   vi

Introduction   1

1. Secret Confession (to God)   6

2. Private Confession (to an offended individual)   18

3. Public Confession (to the church)   31

4. Auricular Confession 1 (to a priest):
   The Minister's Authority   46

5. Auricular Confession 2 (to a priest):
   The Penitent's Need   65

   Conclusion   80

   Appendix: Some Official Anglican Statements   84

   Bibliography   89

   Notes   92

   Subject Index   99

   Scripture Index   104

Foreword

A little book can make a big impact. That is certainly true of *Confess Your Sins: The Way of Reconciliation* by John Stott. Only a little over one hundred pages, the book's message has the power to renew the church today.

John Stott (1921–2011) was one of his generation's premier writers and preachers on biblical themes. His books stood out for their faithfulness to Scripture, clarity of expression, and cogency of reasoning. Never have I read something written by John Stott and walked away unhelped. As for his preaching, Kenneth Kantzer, for many years Dean of Trinity Evangelical Divinity School, wrote this about Stott: "When I hear him expound a text, invariably I exclaim to myself, 'That's exactly what it means! Why didn't I see it before?'" I would say the same.

Preaching at Stott's memorial service, J. I. Packer spoke of "his vision for a renewed church" as one key to his lasting influence. And this is where his wonderful book *Confess Your Sins* fits in. Who of us doesn't sin? And who of us isn't renewed by confession? The value of Stott's book lies in the practical, biblical wisdom with which he guides us into honest confession. For example, on pages 28-29, Stott points out something surprising in Luke 17:3, where our Lord commands us, "If your brother or sister sins against you, rebuke them; and if they repent, forgive them." Stott writes:

We are to rebuke a brother if he sins against us; we are to forgive him if he repents—and only if he repents. We must beware of cheapening forgiveness. . . . If a brother who has sinned against us refuses to repent, we should not forgive him. Does this startle you? It is what Jesus taught. Oh, we must "forgive" him in the sense that our thoughts towards him are free of all animosity and full of love. But this is not Christian forgiveness. "Forgiveness" means more than that; it includes restoration to fellowship. If we can restore to full and intimate fellowship with ourselves a sinning and unrepentant brother, we reveal not the depth of our love, but its shallowness, for we are doing what is not for his highest good. A forgiveness which bypasses the need for repentance issues not from love but from sentimentality.

We can be grateful for Stott's clear-headed reading of the Bible to help us see such an important truth.

After my dad, Dr. Ray Ortlund Sr., died in 2007, I received his theological library. In among the other books was *Confess Your Sins* in its original publication. Opening my dad's copy, I found it generously and meaningfully marked up in my dad's own handwriting. He loved this book, and I have come to love it, too. Stott himself once wrote, "Our favorite books become very precious to us, and we even develop with them an almost living and affectionate relationship." I agree. And I hope you will join me in my affection for John Stott's *Confess Your Sins: The Way of Reconciliation.* What could be greater than a wave of confession and reconciliation washing over us all in our troubled world today?

I thank Eerdmans Publishing Company for bringing this small, high-impact book back to us for a new day of renewal!

RAY C. ORTLUND JR., *Pastor*
Immanuel Church
Nashville, Tennessee

Introduction

The title of this book, *Confess Your Sins,* will no doubt seem to some a clear indication of the unhealthy preoccupation of Christians with their sins. A year or two ago a lay correspondent wrote to *The Times* to complain of this very tendency. He found it disconcerting, whenever he attended a Church of England service, to be reminded of his sins. At Morning and Evening Prayer he was obliged to associate himself with the rest of the congregation as a crowd of "miserable offenders." At every baptism he was informed that he was "conceived and born in sin," at every wedding that marriage was "a remedy against sin," and at every funeral that death delivered men "out of the miseries of this sinful world." He had come to the conclusion that sin was with churchmen a veritable obsession.

There is no need for us to be offended by this criticism. We are not in the least ashamed of the fact that we think and talk a lot about sin. We do so for the simple reason that we are realists. Sin is an ugly fact. It is to be neither ignored nor ridiculed, but honestly faced. Indeed, Christianity is the only religion in the world which takes sin seriously and offers a satisfactory remedy for it. And the way to enjoy this remedy is not to deny the disease, but to confess it.

So far, so good. But to whom should we confess our sins? Some people say that it is necessary to confess them to a priest, and that this is in fact the way which God has appointed for us to be forgiven. Is this so? What is the character of Christian confession and the way of Christian forgiveness?

It may be useful to approach these questions by clearing the ground a bit, and by taking our stand on the common ground which is (or should be) shared by all Christians alike, whatever our particular persuasion. The truths on which we should be able to agree concern the fact and guilt of *sin*, the possibility of *forgiveness*, and the need for *confession*. Sin-confession-forgiveness are, in fact, an inseparable trio. Let me elaborate these truths in three straightforward Christian propositions.

Sin and Guilt

1. Our sins involve us in guilt, so that we need to be forgiven.

I cannot delay to establish the fact of human sin; I must assume that this is not in dispute between us. We have fallen short of our own ideals, let alone God's standards. We have broken our own rules of conduct, let alone God's holy laws. We are sinners.

But we must go further and add that we are *guilty* sinners. This is because sin, according to the Bible, is primarily an offense against God. Its gravity lies here. However much our misdeeds may bring disgrace to ourselves and sorrow and suffering to others, their greatest evil is that they constitute a rebellion against God, our Creator and our Lord. One of the Bible's simplest definitions of sin is that "sin is lawlessness" (1 Jn 3:4). The two words are convertible. Sin is an infringement of God's known will, a revolt against his authority. It therefore makes us "accountable to God" (Rom 3:19), bringing us under his righteous displeasure and judgment. Only divine forgiveness can expunge our guilt and restore us to fellowship with God.

Forgiveness

2. *Forgiveness is offered to us by God on the sole ground of the death of his Son.*

All Christians believe that God is a forgiving God. It is part of our basic creed. "I believe in . . . the forgiveness of sins." Christianity is fundamentally a religion of salvation, and salvation includes forgiveness. Thus one of the great promises of the New Covenant, foretold through Jeremiah, which Jesus said would be ratified by the shedding of his blood, was: "I will forgive their wickedness, and will remember their sins no more" (Jer 31:34; Mt 26:28). When the apostles began to preach the gospel, they were faithful to their Lord's commission and proclaimed forgiveness of sins to those who repented and believed (Lk 24:47; Acts 2:38; 3:19; 13:38–39). What they preached in their sermons, they also wrote in their epistles—for example, as a recognizable echo of Matthew 26:28, that in Christ "we have redemption through his blood, the forgiveness of sins, in accordance with the riches of God's grace" (Eph 1:7).

This last quotation not only makes it plain that redemption and forgiveness are to some extent equivalent terms and that they are a present, conscious possession which in Christ "we have," but that they are both attributable to "his blood," that is to say, his death on the cross. The Scripture teaches that when he died, he "bore our sins" (1 Pt 2:24), an Old Testament expression meaning that he suffered the consequences of our sins, and that only because he was "made . . . to be sin for us" can we "become the righteousness of God," that is, be forgiven and accepted (2 Cor 5:21).

What the Bible asserts, the Prayer Book faithfully reflects. In the Holy Communion service we are told (in the first exhortation) that "we obtain remission of our sins" by "His meritorious Cross and Passion . . . alone." In confessing our sins we therefore pray that God will have mercy upon us and for his "Son our Lord

3

Jesus Christ's sake forgive us all that is past," and in the prayer of oblation, after receiving the sacrament, we pray again that "by the merits and death of Thy Son Jesus Christ, and through faith in His blood, we and all Thy whole Church may obtain remission of *our sins*." We cannot escape this indissoluble link in Bible and Prayer Book between the death of Christ and the forgiveness of our sins. Each of us needs to pray for our soul: "wash it, we pray Thee, in the blood of that immaculate Lamb, that was slain to take away the sins of the world."[1]

Confession

3. The confession of sin is a necessary condition of receiving the forgiveness of God.

The clearest statement of this third proposition is in one of the Scripture sentences which introduces Morning and Evening Prayer: "If we claim to be without sin, we deceive ourselves and the truth is not in us. If we confess our sins, he is faithful and just and will forgive our sins and purify us from all unrighteousness" (1 Jn 1:8–9). Here are two "if" sentences placed in contrast to one another, stating the result on the one hand of denying that we are sinners and on the other of confessing our sins. If we deny our sin, we deceive ourselves; if we confess our sins, we are forgiven. So the forgiveness of sins by God is made conditional upon the confession of sins by man. The Prayer Book exhortation goes on to enforce this truth, that we should "acknowledge and confess our manifold sins and wickedness, and that we should not dissemble, nor cloke them, before the face of Almighty God our heavenly Father, but confess them . . . *to the end that* we may obtain forgiveness of the same." Forgiveness depends on confession.

So much is agreed among us. We are guilty sinners. Our merciful God offers us forgiveness through Jesus Christ. We must

4

confess our sins. But how, and to whom, should our confession be made? This is the question, and a preliminary answer may already be given, because an important principle emerges from the three agreed propositions above. We have seen that they belong together. Sin, forgiveness, and confession cannot be separated. Moreover, confession is the link between sin and its forgiveness, and can for this reason be understood only in relation to the sin that has been committed and the forgiveness that is desired. To be more precise, confession must be made *to* the person *against* whom we have sinned and *from* whom we need and desire to receive forgiveness. Therefore, before we can judge whether it is proper for us to confess our sins to somebody, whether God or man, we must ask two questions. First, have I sinned against him, that I should confess my sin to him? Secondly, has he authority to forgive me that I should ask him to do so?

If we apply this principle, we can immediately distinguish between three different kinds of confession corresponding to three different kinds of sin. There is "secret confession" to God because there are "secret sins" (Ps 90:8) committed against God alone. Next, there is "private confession," because some of our sins are committed against man as well as God, a private individual, or two or three such, and must be confessed to the offended party. Thirdly, there is "public confession," because some sins are committed against a group of people, a community, or the whole local congregation, and must therefore be confessed publicly.

The nature and the necessity of these three kinds of confession will be considered in the first three chapters of this book. We shall then be in a position in the last two chapters to ask: Where does "auricular confession" to a priest fit into this biblical scheme?

CHAPTER ONE

Secret Confession (to God)

The awful dilemma of "to confess" or "not to confess" probably conjures up in our minds some of the most painful recollections of our school days. Some damage has been done to school property. The crime has been discovered, but the culprit has not been caught. The school is paraded. "Who is responsible for this act of vandalism?" The headmaster's voice repeats the question. Tense silence. Somebody is experiencing a bitter inner struggle between duty and fear. The tension is only relieved when at last he owns up.

The adult has the same struggle in his relationship to God. Indeed it has been so ever since man first disobeyed God and fell from his original state of innocence. "They hid from the LORD God among the trees of the garden." "I was afraid," Adam said when God called him, "so I hid." Self-consciously aware of their nakedness (the physical counterpart, no doubt, to a sense of moral shame), Adam and Eve even "sewed fig leaves together and made coverings for themselves" (Gn 3:7–10). It is all very well smiling at their naivety; we too have our aprons of fig leaves, pathetic attempts to cover up, to conceal from God what we know ourselves to be.

The alternative between "covering" our sins and "confessing" them is set before us very clearly in Proverbs 28:13: "Whoever conceals their sins does not prosper, but the one who confesses and renounces them finds mercy." As so often in the book of Proverbs, the contrast is not merely between two opposite courses of action, but between the consequences of each. No one who covers his sins will prosper; it is he who confesses them who will find mercy. What is at stake, we are told, is our spiritual prosperity, whether we receive or forfeit the mercy of God. Many of us are not prospering in our Christian lives. We are making little or no progress. We have got stuck and do not appear to be enjoying the mercy of God. Is the reason partly or wholly that we have neglected the plain teaching of this Scripture about the secret confession of our sins to God?

The Folly of Covering Sin

The practice of covering or concealing sin is characteristic of unbelievers. They neither acknowledge their sins nor feel their guilt or peril. Consequently, they do not cry to God to have mercy on them or flee to Jesus Christ for refuge from the judgment their sins deserve. Indeed, this old-fashioned language means nothing to them. If they heard it, they would laugh at it. But their position is far more serious than they realize. "Whoever conceals their sins does not prosper." They are on the broad road which leads to destruction.

We must not suppose, however, that this verse has no reference to Christian believers. It has. There is a common and dangerous tendency among us to "cover" our sins. We may go to church and join in the general confession, and in our private prayers say we are sorry for our sins. But our words have a hollow sound. Our confession is largely a formality. The truth is that we do more covering up than uncovering. We know little of the uncomfortable discipline of confessing and forsaking our sins and so finding mercy. It is not difficult to rationalize our distaste for it.

Some people would have us believe that the whole idea of confessing sin is morbid and unhealthy. "It's such an unwholesome thing," they say, "to concentrate on your sins; it only adds to the number of neurotics who suffer from a guilt complex." Well, some forms of confession *are* unhealthy, especially if we keep raking over our past which should have been long ago confessed, forsaken, and forgiven. But true confession, the honest, shamefaced uncovering before God of the sins of the past day or week, far from being unhealthy, is an essential condition of spiritual health. It is the person who covers his sins who is unhealthy; he "shall not prosper." There can be no mental or spiritual health without honesty.

The Bible gives us a graphic account of the inner turmoil of a man who tried to cover his sins: "When I kept silent, my bones wasted away through my groaning all day long. For day and night your hand was heavy on me; my strength was sapped as in the heat of summer. Then I acknowledged my sin to you and did not cover up my iniquity. I said, 'I will confess my transgressions to the LORD.' And you forgave the guilt of my sin" (Ps 32:3-5). I could echo these words from my own experience. There is no misery of mind or spirit to compare with estrangement from God through sin and the refusal to confess it in penitence; and there is no joy like fellowship with God through repentance, confession, and forgiveness.

Other people do not confess their sins for a very different reason. They imagine they have no need to do so. They have an unbalanced view of holiness. They suppose they have attained such a degree of perfection that there is nothing left to confess. All one can say to them is that Jesus was not of their opinion. He taught us to pray, "forgive us our trespasses." He evidently did not anticipate a time when his disciples could dispense with this petition. Similarly, the Church of England puts a general confession on our lips every time we come to worship, whether at Morning or Evening Prayer or at Holy Communion. It may indeed be that, by the grace of God, there are days when no actual transgression stains the conscience or memory of the Christian. But still there

8

are sins of omission to confess, for no man has loved God with all his heart, mind, soul, and strength; and there is the infection and corruption of our fallen nature to mourn, as we acknowledge that "there is no health in us."

Yet other people, ready to catch at the flimsiest straw in their desperate anxiety to cover their sins and justify themselves, resort to a biblical argument. "We are *meant* to cover our sins," they say; "the Scriptures themselves plainly teach that 'love covers a multitude of sins.' Didn't you know that this is written several times in the book of Proverbs (10:12; 11:13; 17:9), and twice in the New Testament too (Jas 5:20; 1 Pt 4:8)? It is quite wrong to uncover our sins in the way you are suggesting." I cannot imagine that the reader will be deceived by this. It is easy to misquote Scripture. The devil himself is an expert at it. But these verses have nothing whatever to do with the subject before us. They teach that if we truly love other people, we shall want to cover their sins. We shall not gossip about them, or expose them to criticism or ridicule, but rather seek to lead them to Christ, so that God may forgive them. There is nothing here to dissuade us from uncovering our own sins in secret confession to God.

All these are superficial excuses. They disguise the real reason why we tend to cover our sins before God, which is that we want to conceal them even from ourselves. We cannot bear the humiliation of seeing and facing ourselves as we really are. Such is our innate pride that we prefer fiction to fact. We are in love with the fantasy image of ourselves which we have created, and refuse to escape from our dreamland. It is sheer vanity. We cannot endure the injury to our self-esteem which an honest uncovering and confession of our sins would bring to us. So we try to cover our sins from ourselves and God, so as to leave our comfortable complacency undisturbed. It is this that is unhealthy, the covering of our sins, not the uncovering of them. Such self-deception is ruinous to all spiritual health, for one of the most elementary rules of mental and spiritual health is to know the truth about ourselves and to admit it.

The folly of trying to cover our sins would be hard to exaggerate. "Whoever conceals their sins does not prosper," either in this world or the next.

For one thing, however successful we may be in concealing our sins from ourselves and from others, we cannot conceal them from God. Adam and Eve tried to hide themselves among the trees of the garden, but the Lord God found them there. He knows us as we are, not as we would like to think we are. He knows our secret thoughts, motives, and deceptions. All things are naked and open before him. He is called in the Bible the "heart-knower." We do not, therefore, confess our sins to him to inform him of what he is ignorant, but rather to "acknowledge and bewail" what he already knows.

Not only does God know us as we are now, but one day we are going to be made known as we are. Let me put the same truth in another way: If we cover our sins in this life, they will be uncovered in the next. The Bible tells us that the day of judgment will be an occasion of acute embarrassment for all hypocrites who have covered themselves up. So Jesus said: "There is nothing concealed that will not be disclosed, or hidden that will not be made known. What you have said in the dark will be heard in daylight, and what you have whispered in the ear in the inner rooms will be proclaimed from the roofs" (Lk 12:2–3). We shall not be able to retain any secrets on that dreadful day. We shall be exposed in the poverty-stricken nakedness of our sin, selfishness, and shame. We shall long to escape from this exposure, and the judgment which will follow it, but we shall not be able, even though we cry "to the mountains and the rocks, 'Fall on us and hide us from the face of him who sits on the throne and from the wrath of the Lamb! For the great day of their wrath has come, and who can withstand it?'" (Rv 6:16–17; see also Hos 10:8; Lk 23:30).

It is in these ways that "whoever conceals their sins does not prosper." No lie ever did prosper. To cover our sins is to court spiritual ruin.

The Wisdom of Confessing Sin

If the way to forfeit prosperity is to cover our sins, the way to find mercy is to uncover them, to bring them out of the darkness of secrecy and deception into the burning light of God's presence. Such uncovering of sin before God leads first to confessing it, then to forsaking it, so that we may find mercy. In these two activities, confessing and forsaking, is revealed the double purpose of uncovering our sins.

First, we need to uncover our sins in order that God may forgive them. I referred earlier in this chapter to Psalm 32, in which we are given a graphic description of the pain of covering our sins. The same psalm describes the joy of the man "in whose spirit is no deceit," who does not deceive himself but confesses his sin, so that God forgives or "covers" it. There is a deliberate contrast and play on words between these two experiences. The psalmist writes: "Blessed is the one whose transgressions are forgiven, whose sins are covered" (v. 1), and later: "I acknowledged my sin to you and did not cover up my iniquity" (v. 5). The words "covered" and "cover up" in these verses translate the same Hebrew verb. It means to "cover" in the sense of to conceal. It is used of clothes covering the body and a veil covering the face, of water covering the earth and the clouds covering the sun; and it occurs metaphorically in Psalm 32 both of *men* covering their sins in a refusal to confess them, and of *God* covering their sins by his merciful forgiveness.[1] Indeed, the two are alternatives. As soon as David uncovered his sins, God covered them, for God can only cover with his forgiveness the sins which we uncover in our confession. It is God's loving desire to cover our sins, to "blot out" our transgressions, to put them from us as far as the east is from the west, to cast them behind his back, to bury them in the depths of the sea, to remember them no more. These are the vivid expressions found in the Bible for the forgiveness of sins.[2] Happy indeed is the man who has experienced this forgiveness! The relief and joy are indescribable.

But this covering of sin is for him to do, not for us. Some people foolishly try to cover their own sins, to forget them, only to find that they continue to haunt them. The means which God has appointed for the putting away of sins is that we should deliberately recall them and bring them out with shame into the open, and let him cover them through the merit of his Son's death.

The reason why we are to uncover our sins is not only that God may forgive them, but that we may forsake them. There is a closer link than we often realize between the confessing of sins and the forsaking of them. How can we expect to overcome in the future if we do not deal seriously with our failures of the past?

One of the greatest snares to which Christians are exposed in the contemporary world is the tendency to grow accustomed to sin. It is not just that sin is ingrained in our nature, or that the devil refuses to leave us alone, but that the influences of "the world," the pressures of a godless, secular society, are so insidious. Wherever we look, sin stares us in the face. The standards of the press, radio, television, and advertisements are, to say the least, sub-Christian. We cannot escape this continuous assault upon us. It is frighteningly easy to become morally insensitive, and to find that we are no longer hurt or grieved or shocked by the evil with which we are surrounded.

One of the surest antidotes to this process of moral hardening is the disciplined practice of uncovering our sins of thought and outlook, as well as of word and deed, and the repentant forsaking of them. It is not enough to confess them, asking for forgiveness and cleansing; we need deliberately, definitely, specifically to forsake them. We would not be so plagued by "besetting sins" if we did this. It is important, when we bring our sins into the open before God, not to stop there, but to go on to adopt a right attitude towards both God and the sin itself. First, we confess the sin, humbling ourselves with a contrite heart before God. Secondly, we forsake it, rejecting and repudiating it. This is a vital part of what is meant by "mortification" in the New Testament. It is taking up towards sin an attitude of resolute antagonism. The uncovering of sin is in itself of little value; it must lead us to an attitude both of humility towards God and of hostility towards sin. "Let those who love the LORD hate evil," or "the LORD loves those who hate evil" (RSV) (Ps 97:10); and it is this holy hatred of evil which is promoted by the faithful, systematic uncovering and confession of our sins.

Is It Really Necessary?

There are two important objections to this practice of secret confession to God which need to be considered at this stage. The first concerns the question why we should confess our sins *to God*. "Why should I confess all my sins to him?" someone asks. "I admit that I am sometimes beastly to other people and that I ought to apologize to *them*; but what has it got to do with God?" This may sound a reasonable objection, but not if we accept the biblical view of sin which has already been outlined in the Introduction. The Bible views sin as being fundamentally "lawlessness," whether positively or negatively. It is both a "transgression," the stepping over a forbidden boundary, a "trespass" into territory where we have no right to be, and also a "missing the mark," a failure to do what we should do or be what we should be. In either case, an absolute moral standard is implied, whether we are said to break it or to fail to attain it. And this moral standard is God's law. Therefore, even if our sins are an offense to our fellow men, because we hate them or envy them or are rude or unkind to them, they are also a sin against God, because they are a breach of his great commandment: "Thou shalt love thy neighbor as thyself."

The most striking example of this is David's sin with Bathsheba, which probably lies behind the confession of Psalm 51. He saw her bathing and was attracted by her beauty, lusted after her, took her for himself, had a child by her, and arranged for her husband to be killed in battle. One after another he broke four of the last five commandments: he coveted, he stole, he committed adultery, he murdered. And yet, when through the ministry of the prophet Nathan he was brought to repentance, he cried: "Against you, you only, have I sinned and done what is evil in your sight" (Ps 51:4). This is not a denial that he had sinned against Bathsheba, against her lawful husband, and against the whole nation of which he was king; but it is a recognition that all sins are first and foremost a defiance of the holy laws of God.

True confession is, therefore, not merely an admission that I have sinned, but that I have sinned *against God*. The compilers of the Book of Common Prayer were quite clear about this and make us acknowledge it when we confess our sins in church. "We have . . . strayed *from Thy ways* like lost sheep. . . . We have offended *against Thy holy laws*. . . . We acknowledge and bewail our manifold sins and wickedness, which we, from time to time most grievously have committed, by thought, word, and deed, *against Thy Divine Majesty*." It is because we are "miserable offenders" in this sense, having defied God's authority and broken his laws, that we have "provoked most justly His wrath and indignation against us." "He it is that is offended with us," wrote Bullinger "and therefore of Him we must desire forgiveness"[3] and, further, to him we must confess our sins.

"But," a second objector may now say, "what is this confession, which you are making a condition of forgiveness? I have always understood that we are 'justified by faith alone'; aren't you guilty of destroying the Reformation principle of *sola fides* by adding another condition of salvation?" This is an important argument to consider, although it is not difficult to answer. Justification is indeed through faith alone. It is God's acceptance of the sinner, on the sole ground of Christ's death for his sins, when by faith he lays hold of Christ as his Savior. But no man ever thus believes in Christ who has not first acknowledged his need. And our need of Christ's salvation is found in our sin and guilt. This is why repentance is so often coupled with faith in Bible and Prayer Book. "Repent and believe the good news" was the message of Jesus and his apostles;[4] forgiveness is granted to those who "truly repent and unfeignedly believe His holy gospel" (the absolution). Turning trustfully to Jesus Christ for deliverance presupposes a recognition of our sin and a renunciation of it. And confession is simply a part of repentance. We have already seen in Proverbs 28:13 how "confessing and renouncing" belong together. Similarly, in the general confession we pray: "Spare Thou them, O God, which *confess* their faults. Restore Thou them that are *penitent*." Bible and Prayer Book know nothing of a formal confession in words which is not the expression of a "humble, lowly, penitent, and obedient heart" (the exhortation).

It is in this connection that something needs to be said about the twofold use of the word "confess" in the New Testament, first the confession of sin, and secondly the confession of faith in God and in Jesus Christ. Often they occur quite separately and independently,[5] but sometimes they are in significant association.[6] As Charles Biber has written, "These are the two aspects of one and the same revolution: Jesus Christ came, indeed, to bring the forgiveness of sins."[7] It is inconceivable that the Christian should ever think of sin without also thinking of his Savior. Humble confession of the one leads to thankful confession of the other. The confession of sin is not, therefore, an additional condition of salvation; it is itself an integral part of true, saving faith in Christ.

A Practical Plea

In view of all this plain biblical teaching regarding the necessity of confessing our sins, let me plead that we should take it more seriously and be more disciplined in it. In particular, the Christian's confession of sin should be both immediate and detailed.

It is a great mistake to imagine that, when we are conscious of having sinned, we must wait, before confessing it, until the following Sunday or Holy Communion service, or even until our time of prayer that night. The apostle Paul affirmed before Felix: "So I strive always to keep my conscience clear before God and man" (Acts 24:16). We should have the same ambition. As soon as any sin is on our conscience, whether committed against God or men, we must confess it. This is what it means to "walk in the light" (1 Jn 1:7). It has been described as living in a house without ceiling or walls—permitting no barrier to arise between us and either God or our fellows. It is a very serious thing to tamper with our conscience or to let it remain burdened and unrelieved. As soon as we have sinned against our neighbor we should apologize. As soon as we are conscious of God's face having become clouded, so that we are estranged from him, we need to get away quietly, to uncover our sin, to confess and forsake it. As Thomas Becon, Archbishop Cranmer's chaplain, put it: "This kind of confession ought every Christian man daily and hourly to make unto God, so oft as he is brought unto the knowledge of his sin."[8] It is an indispensable condition of abiding continuously in Christ.

Our confession must also be detailed. An omnibus confession is not enough: "O God, I'm sorry for my sins. Amen." Such a general confession may be suitable for public worship in church; in private devotion our confession must be particular. The biblical promise of divine forgiveness is made to those who confess their "sins" in the plural (1 Jn 1:9). I believe this should always be part of our response to God's Word after we have read the Bible, for the Bible is not only a revelation of God's Name, calling us to worship and faith, but a revelation of man's sin, calling us to repentance and confession. What sin has been exposed in the passage we read this morning? Whatever it is, it lurks in our heart. If it has erupted in sinful thoughts, words, or deeds, we must confess them. The other time in which to be specific in confession is at night. Do we not look back over the day to recall God's mercies, so that we "forget not all his benefits," and thank him for them one by one? We must also look back over the day, asking the Holy Spirit to search us and to remind and convict us of our sins, so that we can uncover them in humility before God one by one. I must insist again that this is not morbid introspection, provided that the discovering and uncovering of our sins are not an end in themselves. We must never look back at our past sins or into our wicked hearts without immediately looking away from them in repentance and up to Jesus Christ in faith. The whole purpose of uncovering our sins is that we go on first to confess them, asking for cleansing through the blood of Christ, and then to forsake them, praying for grace to overcome.

Another time for detailed confession is before and at Holy Communion to which we come seeking in a special way forgiveness through the death of Christ (1 Cor 11:28, 31). The first and third exhortations urge us before we come to examine ourselves "through the law" (see Rom 3:20). We continue this private self-examination in public when the Ten Commandments are read, first confessing our infringement of each ("Lord, have mercy upon us"), and then praying for grace to obey it in future ("and incline our hearts to keep this law"). It would be a sad day if this recitation of the commandments at Holy Communion were to be generally abandoned.

Such confessing and forsaking, immediate and detailed, are required of every Christian. It is a question of honesty versus hypocrisy. The uncovering of sins is painful and humiliating. It brings us to our knees in lowliness before God. But if we want to receive mercy, both forgiveness for the past and power for the future, there is no other way. Let it never be said of us that we take sin lightly or presume on the mercy of God.

CHAPTER TWO

Private Confession (to an offended individual)

We have considered the necessity of confessing our sins secretly to God. We have sinned against him and must confess our sins to him, if we desire him to forgive us. This is plain. But is there any biblical warrant for confessing our sins also to a fellow man? Yes, there is. Although all misdeeds are sins against God, some are sins against men as well; and when our sin has offended men as well as God, we must confess to them and seek forgiveness from them too. We have to say to the injured party, in the prodigal's words to his father: "I have sinned against heaven *and against you*" (Lk 15:18, 21). The principle is clear. Let William Tyndale state it for us: "To whom a man trespasseth, unto him he ought to confess."[1] We must seek forgiveness from him whom we have offended; we must confess to him from whom we seek forgiveness.

Indeed, the Bible lays great emphasis on the importance of right relations with our fellow men, teaching that a right relationship with God is impossible without them. The great Hebrew prophets of the seventh and eighth centuries B.C. constantly reiterated this theme. The offering of sacrifices to God was not only useless, but positively nauseating to him, they said, if the worshippers were living lives of immorality or injustice to men. "Stop bringing meaningless offerings! . . . Your New Moon feasts and your appointed festivals I hate with all my being. . . . When you spread out you hands in prayer, I hide my eyes from you; even when you offer many prayers, I am not listening. Your hands are full of blood! Wash and make yourselves clean. Take your evil deeds out of my sight; stop doing wrong. Learn to do right; seek justice. Defend the oppressed. Take up the cause of the fatherless; plead the case of the widow" (Is 1:13–17).[2]

Granted that right relations with their fellow men are necessary for the people of God, what are they to do when these relationships go wrong? It may be helpful to distinguish between three separate duties—confession, restitution, and rebuke.

Confession

If we have sinned against our neighbor, we must confess our sin to him and ask for his forgiveness. It sounds easy; yet we all know from common experience how costly it is simply to apologize to somebody and to say that we are sorry. It is a rare Christian grace. D. L. Moody, the famous American evangelist of the last century, exhibited it, and I think I was more struck by this than by anything else about him when reading a recent biography. Let me give you two examples which impressed me. In the early days at their home in Northfield, Massachusetts, Moody was anxious to have a lawn like those he had greatly admired in England. But one day his two sons, Paul and Will, let the horses loose from the barn. They galloped over his precious lawn and ruined it. And Moody lost his temper with them. But the boys never forgot how, after they had gone to bed that night, they heard his heavy footsteps as he approached and entered their room, and, laying a heavy hand on their head, said to them: "I want you to forgive me; that wasn't the way Christ taught."[3] On another occasion a theological student interrupted him during an address and Moody snapped an irritated retort. Let J. C. Pollock describe what happened at the end of the sermon: "He reached his close. He paused. Then he said: 'Friends, I want to confess before you all that I made a great mistake at the beginning of this meeting. I answered my young brother down there foolishly. I ask God to forgive me. I ask *him* to forgive me.'" And before anyone realized what was happening, the world's most famous evangelist had stepped off the platform, dashed across to the insignificant, anonymous youth, and taken him by the hand. As another present said, "The man of iron will proved that he had mastered the hardest of all earth's languages, 'I am sorry.'" Someone else called it "the greatest thing I ever saw D. L. Moody do."[4]

Perhaps a word of caution may be written here. All sins, whether of thought, word, or deed, must be confessed to God, because he sees them all. "You have searched me, LORD, and you know me. You know when I sit and when I rise; you perceive my thoughts from afar. You discern my going out and my lying down; you are familiar with all my ways. Before a word is on my tongue you, LORD, know it completely." (Ps 139:1–4). But we need to remember that men do not share the omniscience of God. They hear our words and see our works; they cannot read our hidden thoughts. It is, therefore, social sins of word and deed which we must confess to our fellow men, not the sinful thoughts we may have harbored about them. Some zealous believers, in their anxiety to be open and honest, go too far in this matter. To say "I'm sorry I was rude to you" or "I'm sorry I showed off in front of you" is right; but not "I'm afraid I've had jealous thoughts about you all day." Such a confession does not help; it only embarrasses. If the sin remains secret in the mind and does not erupt into words or deeds, it must be confessed to God alone. It is true that, according to the teaching of Jesus, "anyone who looks at a woman lustfully has already committed adultery with her in his heart" (Mt 5:28); but this is adultery *in the sight of God* and is to be confessed to him, not to her. The rule is always that secret sins must be confessed secretly (to God), and private sins must be confessed privately (to the injured party).

The clearest teaching in the New Testament about such private confession came from the lips of our Lord himself, in the course of the Sermon on the Mount: "Therefore, if you are offering your gift at the altar and there remember that your brother or sister has something against you, leave your gift there in front of the altar. First go and be reconciled to them; then come and offer your gift" (Mt 5:23–24). The situation is obvious. We are going to church, and on the way we suddenly remember somebody who has a grievance against us. It is not that he has wronged us, but we him. The teaching of Jesus is clear. It is no use going to church when such a sin comes to our mind and burdens our conscience. We cannot draw near to God while we are estranged from a brother. The command is: "first go . . .; then come." First "be reconciled to them" (which means ask for his forgiveness), and then your offering will be acceptable to God.

This need to be "in love and charity with our neighbors" is much insisted upon in the Prayer Book. It is an indispensable condition of coming to the Lord's Supper: "And if ye shall perceive your offences to be such as are not only against God, but also against your neighbors; then ye shall reconcile yourselves unto them" (first exhortation). Similarly, in the Visitation of the Sick, the minister is to examine the sick person whether he "be in charity with all the world, exhorting him to forgive, from the bottom of his heart, all persons that have offended him, and if he hath offended any other, to ask them forgiveness."

It seems appropriate at this point to mention the command of St. James: " Therefore confess your sins to each other and pray for each other so that you may be healed" (5:16). There is certainly here no reference whatever to the practice of auricular confession to a priest, despite the fact that "the elders of the church" (5:14), whom the sick person is to send for, are in the Rhemish New Testament of 1582 inaccurately labelled "priests"! Commentators have rightly pointed out that if auricular confession is in view, then the priest must confess to the penitent as well as the penitent to the priest, since the confession is to be reciprocal "one to another."[5]

Nor do I think there is a reference here to the reciprocal, private confession of secret sins, because the biblical principle is consistently that "confession" is due to the party who has been offended. Thus, sins against man are confessed to God and man, since they are committed against both. But sins against God are *confessed* to God alone and not to man, since they are *committed* against God alone and not man. The great sixteenth-century Swiss theologian, Heinrich Bullinger, was surely right in interpreting this verse as a command to those who have "mutually offended one another" to confess these sins to one another.[6] It suits the context too, that physical healing may be hindered by a breach of fellowship with our fellow men.

Restitution

Real repentance often involves restitution. True, in sins committed against God no restitution of any kind is possible; we can only worship him that, on the ground of the death of his Son for our sins, he is ready to blot out fully and freely all our transgressions. But in some sins against men we can make restitution, and when we can we must.

This whole issue became very confused in the Middle Ages through the so-called sacrament of penance, and we need to understand the changes which the Reformation brought. In the article on "penance" in the *Oxford Dictionary of the Christian Church*, it is conceded that of its early history "very little is known." It seems to be clear, however, that the first use of penance was public, not private. The commination service starts with the statement that "in the Primitive Church there was a godly discipline, that, at the beginning of Lent, such persons as stood convicted of notorious sin were put to open penance." That is, open penance was the penalty for open sin. These "penitents" were only restored to communion after a period of submission to strenuous discipline in prayer, fasting, and almsgiving. As Hooker put it, "The course of discipline in former ages reformed open transgressors by putting them unto offices of open penitence, especially confession, whereby they declared their own crimes in the hearing of the whole church."[7] Hooker goes on to explain how, when such "public confessions became dangerous and prejudicial to the safety of well-minded men and . . . advantageous to the enemies of God's Church,"[8] they were gradually superseded by a system of private confession, whose purpose was concerned with discipline, not absolution, however. Penitential books were published from about the fifth century in which a catalog of sins was supplied with suitable penances. The Fourth Lateran Council of 1215 made private confession and penance compulsory for every Christian at least once a year.

The medieval schoolmen went further and developed their elaborate sacrament of penance, which consisted of three parts— contrition, confession, and satisfaction. It is the last of these which concerns us now, for "satisfaction" was regarded as an attempt to make amends for sin, an act of restitution to the injured party. The schoolmen taught that the sinner could and must make some satisfaction to God for his sins. They distinguished between the *culpa* (guilt) of sin and the *poena* (penalty) of sin. They agreed that the satisfaction of Christ on the cross was sufficient to deliver the penitent from the *culpa* of sin, but not from the *poena*. The "eternal" *poena* had to be removed by the sinner's penance, while the "temporal" *poena* would only be finally paid off by the pains of a fiery purgatory, unless it was remitted earlier by the purchase of indulgences.

This dreadful doctrine the Reformers vigorously attacked as being derogatory to the death of Christ. They insisted that all the consequences of sin may be put away by his death. "God forgiveth us both the pain and the guiltiness of sins," cried Latimer in one of his eloquent sermons.[9] Cranmer's prayer of consecration insists that Christ on the cross made "(by his one oblation of himself

23

once offered) a full, perfect, and sufficient sacrifice, oblation, and satisfaction, for the sins of the whole world." Article XXXI adds: "and there is none other satisfaction for sin, but that alone."[10] While denying that sinners could make any satisfaction for their sins to God, or needed to since Christ had done it fully and finally in his death, the Reformers qualified their dismissal of the medieval notion of satisfaction in two respects. First, they emphasized the necessity of true "penitence" as opposed to "penance" and of good works in the life of the penitent believer. He cannot "make amends" to God for his sins; but he can and must "amend his life." His good works are not "meritorious." They "cannot put away sins" or earn his salvation. "Yet are they pleasing and acceptable to God in Christ, and do spring out necessarily of a true and lively faith."[11] They may be said to "satisfy" God only in the sense that they are pleasing to him, not because they atone for sin or win his favor. Similarly, the Christian believer may be called upon to suffer, but his sufferings have no redeeming merit like the sufferings of Christ; their value lies in their power to promote within him holiness, humility, faith, and patience.

Secondly, the Reformers fully agreed that, although no satisfaction could be made for sins against God, the case was very different with sins against men, both corporately and individually. They wanted the restoration of ecclesiastical discipline, with public penance and confession. Jewel urges it in the *Defence of the Apology* as "necessary for the satisfaction of the Church."[12] They also stressed the need to "satisfy," that is, make restitution to an offended brother: "Thou must make him amends or satisfaction, or, at the leastway, if thou be not able, ask him forgiveness."[13] The Book of Common Prayer contains the same requirement: "Ye shall reconcile yourselves unto them (s.c. your offended neighbors), being ready to make restitution and satisfaction, according to the uttermost of your powers, for all injuries and wrongs done by you to any other" (Holy Communion, first exhortation). Similarly, in the Visitation of the Sick, the minister is to exhort the sick person not only to forgive others and ask their forgiveness, as we have seen, but also "where he hath done injury or wrong to any man, that he make amends to the uttermost of his power."

This Prayer Book emphasis is thoroughly biblical. Already in the Law of Moses we find restitution demanded: "Any man or woman who wrongs another in any way and so is unfaithful to the LORD is guilty and must confess the sin they have committed. They must make full restitution for the wrong they have done, add a fifth of the value to it and give it all to the person they have wronged" (Nm 5:6–7). The chief difference between the sin offering and the trespass offering (RSV "guilt offering") seems to have lain here, that the latter was the divine provision for social sins and had to be accompanied by restitution: "when they sin in any of these ways and realize their guilt, they must return what they have stolen or taken by extortion, or what was entrusted to them, or the lost property they found, or whatever it was they swore falsely about. They must make restitution in full, add a fifth of the value to it and give it all to the owner on the day they present their guilt offering" (Lv 6:4–5).

In the New Testament, Zacchaeus, the dishonest tax collector of Jericho, stands out as one of the most striking examples of restitution (Lk 19:1–10). When Jesus brought salvation to his house, he was not content to add to the stolen money which he resolved to return the one-fifth that the law required. He promised the Lord that he would restore *fourfold* the money of which he had defrauded people. He said he would go further even than that. No doubt because there were many of his ill-fated customers whom he could never trace and therefore never repay, he proposed an equivalent: "Look, Lord! Here and now I give half my possessions to the poor." In this way he was willing "to make satisfaction unto all them that he had done injury and wrong unto."[14] This man meant business in his dealings with God. He was beginning a new life through Jesus. He knew perfectly well that his lifelong dishonesty could never be forgiven if he continued to live on the proceeds.

This moral issue is as live today as it was in the days of Moses or during the ministry of Jesus. Those sins which we have committed against man as well as God can never be forgiven if we do not make amends to the utmost of our ability to those we have offended. There may be some stolen money or property to return, some damage to repair, an evil and false report to contradict, a lie to repudiate, or a broken relationship to mend. We must be realistic and practical about this. It is plain logic. Our sins have devastating consequences. Their effects upon God and his law only he can remedy; their effects upon men we can sometimes remedy ourselves. Without such restitution, divine forgiveness is impossible.

Rebuke and Restoration

Wrong relationships can be reciprocal. So far we have concentrated on the injuries we have done to others; what about the injuries which others have done to us? The Bible declares that we have a duty in this matter too. We have to confess and make restitution to those we have wronged, that they may forgive us; we have also to seek to bring to repentance those who have wronged us, that we may forgive them. This is a widely neglected duty. Most of us are as irresponsible as Cain in imagining that we are not our brother's keeper.

The obligation to administer a rebuke to sinners does not rest only upon prophets like John the Baptist (Lk 3:19) or Christian leaders like Timothy and Titus (1 Tm 5:20; 2 Tm 4:2; Ti 1:13; 2:15); it rests upon all Christian believers (Eph 5:11). It is a ministry on which much valuable teaching is given in the book of Proverbs. The contrast which is drawn in this book between the portraits of the wise man and the fool is particularly sharp in this matter.

It is characteristic of the "wise son" that he listens to instruction, admonition, and rebuke, and heeds them (13:1; 15:31). He knows that this is the way to "gain understanding" (15:32; 19:25). He realizes that the reprover rebukes him for his good, out of love for him, and that "better is open rebuke than hidden love" (27:5). He therefore prefers rebuke to flattery (28:23), and even loves the man who reproves him (9:8). The "mocker," on the other hand, refuses to listen to rebuke, and both hates and insults the one who seeks to correct him (9:7, 8; 13:1). He is as stupid to reject reproof as the wise man is prudent to welcome it (12:1; 15:15), for in refusing reproof he goes yet further astray (10:17). Indeed, "whoever remains stiff-necked after many rebukes will suddenly be destroyed—without remedy" (29:1); and "the one who hates correction will die" (15:10).

This teaching in the book of Proverbs is concerned largely with how to *receive* reproof; Jesus taught us how to *give* it. One of his instructions, which is more commonly disregarded and disobeyed than others, is found in Matthew 18:15: "If your brother or sister sins, go and point out their fault, just between the two of you. If they listen to you, you have won them over." "If your brother or sister sins" is a pretty common experience. We have probably all done it to others, and had others do it to us. What do we do when a fellow Christian sins against us? Sometimes we harbor resentment or even begin to plot our revenge. These things are always wrong. At other times we do nothing and imagine ourselves to be fine Christians for overlooking the fault. But Jesus told us there was something for us to do: "Go and point out their fault." There is no need to gossip about him, or to nurse our self-pity by attracting the pity of others. No. "Go and point out their fault, *just between the two of you.*" Just as, when we have offended somebody, we confess our sin to him privately, so when somebody has offended us, we are to approach him about it privately. It is not necessary at this stage for anybody else to know.

Notice next that our purpose in speaking to him privately is clearly defined. It is to "win" him. It is not to humiliate him, but to win him. This is important. There are those who try to avoid the responsibility of this verse by quoting what Jesus said about the "speck" and the "plank" (Mt 7:1–5). They imagine that our Lord was prohibiting altogether the attempt to remove specks out of other people's eyes! He was doing nothing of the kind. What he was condemning was the spirit of proud, hypocritical superiority, when we busy ourselves with the specks in the eyes of others and are blind or indifferent to the planks in our own. He concluded: "You hypocrite, first take the plank out of your own eye, and then you will see clearly to remove the speck from your brother's eye." We must indeed be more critical of ourselves than we are of others, but we cannot shelve our responsibility towards other people in this way. It is our God-given duty to go to a brother who has sinned against us and to tell him his fault, not out of pride, but out of love, "gently" (Gal 6:1). We desire to "win" him (Mt 18:15), to "restore" him (Gal 6:1), to "save" him (Jas 5:19–20). If our purpose is thus constructive, and our spirit meek, an apparently perilous activity will become safe.

A great deal of tension in Christian congregations would be eased if we obeyed this plain command of Jesus: "Go and tell him his fault between you and him alone." Instead of having the courage to face a person with his fault, frankly but privately, we whisper behind his back and poison other people's minds against him. The whole atmosphere of the church becomes foul. The best way to open the windows and let in some fresh air is to do what our Lord commanded: to go and tell him his fault privately, and otherwise to keep our lips sealed. If he listens to us, we shall have "gained" him; a real victory will have been won for Christ and his cause. What we are to do if he does not listen to us belongs to the next chapter.

In Luke 17:3–4 similar teaching of Jesus is recorded, but with a significant addition: "If your brother or sister sins against you, rebuke them; and if they repent, forgive them. Even if they sin against you seven times in a day and seven times come back to you saying 'I repent,' you must forgive them." The passage in St. Matthew's Gospel concentrates on *rebuking* a brother; this passage in St. Luke concentrates rather on *forgiving* him. We are to rebuke a brother if he sins against us; we are to forgive him if he repents—and only if he repents. We must beware of cheapening forgiveness. Although God's forgiveness of us and our forgiveness of one another are quite different (since God is God, and we are merely private individuals, and sinners besides), yet both are conditional upon repentance. If a brother who has sinned against us refuses to repent, we should not forgive him. Does this startle you? It is what Jesus taught. Oh, we must "forgive" him in the sense that our thoughts towards him are free of all animosity and full of love. But this is not Christian forgiveness. "Forgiveness" means more than that; it includes restoration to fellowship. If we can restore to full and intimate fellowship with ourselves a sinning and unrepentant brother, we reveal not the depth of our love but its shallowness, for we are doing what is not for his highest good. A forgiveness which bypasses the need for repentance issues not from love but from sentimentality.

But "if they repent, forgive them." Yes, and "seventy-seven times" (Mt 18:22), for, as Jesus goes on to teach in the parable of the unmerciful servant, how can we refuse to forgive the little debts which others owe us when God has freely forgiven us "all that debt," which we owed him? The parable turns on the comparative size of the debts. The greater our awareness of the magnitude of our sin and of God's forgiveness, the more the sins of others against us will be eclipsed. God will not forgive us if we do not forgive others; for if we do not forgive others, it is evident that we have never seen our own sins as they are and therefore have never truly repented (Mt 6:12–15; Mk 11:25).

God's purpose for his people, as revealed in his Word, is that we should live in harmony with himself and with each other. We are called to peace (Col 3:15). We are to seek peace and to pursue it (1 Pt 3:11). Christianity is in essence a religion of peace and of reconciliation. Therefore we must take seriously every situation in which fellowship is marred or broken. So far as it depends on *us*, we are to live peaceably with all men, and to remember the special blessing which Jesus pronounced upon peacemakers (Mt 5:9; Rom 12:18). We can "make peace" both by confessing our faults to those against whom we have sinned, and by reproving, in order to "restore," those who have sinned against us. But if these activities are truly to promote peace, they must both be kept entirely private.

CHAPTER THREE

Public Confession (to the church)

"Three kinds of confession are expressed unto us in the Scriptures," wrote the great John Jewel, Bishop of Salisbury from 1559, in his *Defence of the Apology*: "The first made secretly unto God alone; the second openly before the whole congregation; the third privately unto our brother."[1] We have already considered secret confession to God and private confession to an offended individual; we must now turn to the subject of public confession to the church.

There are three forms which this public confession may be said to take, although, as I hope to show, the first two forms are public and open without, strictly speaking, being "confession to the church."

General and Formal Confession

The prayer books of the Anglican Communion all contain a formal general confession both in the Holy Communion service and in the services of Morning and Evening Prayer. The pattern of the penitential introduction, consisting of Scripture sentences, exhortation, general confession, and absolution, has been universally recognized as fitting, inasmuch as the people of God may not presume to approach God in worship until they have first been cleansed and forgiven. "It is impossible that a sinner should truly draw near to God in the name of Christ without such a sense of his corruption and guilt being awakened within him as to make him introduce and intersperse his prayer with confession of sin and lamentation on account of it," says Alexander Whyte in his *Commentary on the Shorter Catechism* of the Church of Scotland. "Let the student pass his mind over the record of Scripture, and mark how universal and how acceptable this state of mind was in God's people."[2]

The general confession of Anglican worship is so called because it is intended for the use of all, and is an acknowledgment rather of our general sinfulness than of particular sins. It gives a true and comprehensive description of our sinful condition, in six short sentences. We have strayed from God's ways like lost sheep (an echo of Is 53:6), and offended against his laws. This departure from his ways and infringement of his laws is due to "the devices and desires of our own hearts," which are prone to lead us astray and which "we have followed too much." Our sins are sins of omission as well as commission, concerning not only what we have "done" but what we have "left undone." We are obliged to conclude that "there is no health in us." That is, our sin is not to be measured in deeds alone, but in the disease of our fallen nature. So we are "miserable offenders," which means, offenders in need of the pity of God. We therefore address him as "most merciful" as well as "almighty," and cry to him to have mercy on us who repent and confess our sins. We deserve only to be condemned, but we pray that he will both "spare" us and "restore" us, our only confidence being in his promises given to us through Jesus Christ. Finally, we look beyond our promised forgiveness and pray for grace to live lives of holiness towards God, others, and ourselves ("godly, righteous, and sober"), to the glory of his Name.

In his *Small Catechism* Luther distinguishes two parts of confession: first, the actual confession of sins, and second, the reception of absolution. Absolution, however, is not indiscriminate: it applies only where there is genuine repentance and faith. Thus in the Anglican Prayer Book the minister proclaims that God "pardoneth and absolveth all them that truly repent and unfeignedly believe His holy Gospel"; and the Wurtemberg Confession declares: "Seeing that God promises unto us His free mercy for Christ His Son's sake, and requires of us that we should obediently believe the Gospel of His Son, He also requires that we should mortify the doubting of the flesh and have an assured trust in His mercy" (ch. 14, *Concerning Confession*). Public confession which is merely an outward formality, unrelated to inward contrition and trust, has no part in the absolution and forgiveness of God which the minister pronounces.

Special and Informal Confession

If the general confession is a formal and public acknowledgment to God of our *general* sinfulness, is there any room for the public confession of *specific* sins?

One or two biblical precedents have been advanced for this practice. The first belongs to the ministry of John the Baptist. Large numbers of people from Judea flocked to him at the river Jordan. They listened to his preaching and were baptized by him, "confessing their sins" (Mt 3:6 = Mk 1:5). We are given no information about what form this public confession took. It may have been couched in entirely general terms. On the other hand, since John preached "a baptism of repentance for the forgiveness of sins" (Mk 1:4 = Lk 3:3), and since he applied his teaching in a very detailed and practical way to different classes of people, specifying the "fruit in keeping with repentance" which they were to bear (Lk 3:8, 10–14), it is at least possible that their public confession was more precise than general. This was certainly the case in Ephesus when, as a result of Paul's teaching and certain supernatural happenings, new believers "came and openly confessed what they had done" and made a bonfire of their books of magic (Acts 19:18–19).

These two incidents are similar. It is significant that in neither case is it stated to whom the confession was made, for neither was strictly a "confession" to an injured party (whether God or men), but rather the public "acknowledgment" of the sinfulness of a past life. Each marks a unique occasion, not a habitual practice. John the Baptist was summoning the people to prepare for the coming of the kingdom, and the apostle Paul was bidding them enter it. Such a new beginning involved a drastic renunciation of all that belonged to the past. It included a public confession, and at Ephesus a public burning of evil objects associated with the past, much as converts from heathenism today will express their conversion by publicly burning their idols. Similarly, Dr. B. G. M. Sundkler states that in the Zionist Church initiation ceremonies in South Africa, which he describes as "essentially purgative," "baptism or purification cannot take place without being preceded by confession of sins."[3]

If the public confessions which took place at Jordan under the ministry of John the Baptist and at Ephesus under the ministry of St. Paul were exceptional, marking the beginning of a new life, there is only one biblical reference left which could imply the practice of habitual public confession. This is James 5:16: "Therefore confess your sins to each other and pray for each other so that you may be healed." I have already suggested in the previous chapter that this alludes to the duty of confessing our sins to those we have offended. That the reciprocal confession envisaged is private rather than public is further implied by the immediate mention of an individual "righteous man" whose "effectual fervent prayer . . . availeth much." Nevertheless, reliable commentators have taken the verse to justify the practice of reciprocal confession in public, or at least in small groups. According to the *Second Book of Homilies*, "the true meaning" of this command is "that the faithful ought to acknowledge their offences, whereby some hatred, rancor, grudge, or malice have risen or grown among them, one to another, that a brotherly reconciliation may be had," and our

Lord's words in Matthew 5:23–24 are then quoted as an example. But an alternative explanation is added, "that we ought to confess our weakness and infirmities one to another, to the end that, knowing each other's frailness, we may the more earnestly pray together unto Almighty God, our heavenly Father, that he will vouchsafe to pardon us our infirmities for his Son Jesus Christ's sake."[4]

It is certainly true, if we turn from the Bible to church history, that many movements of the Holy Spirit have been accompanied by this kind of informal reciprocal confession in public. It was a feature of Methodism from the earliest days. The fourth rule of the "bands" (into which the "classes" were subdivided) was "to speak each of us in order, freely and plainly, the true state of our soul, with the faults we have committed in thought, word, or deed, and the temptations we have felt since our last meeting."[5] To John Wesley himself this custom, which characterized the class meetings, was a natural expression of "speaking the truth in love" (Eph 4:15). It had wholesome results. "Many were delivered from the temptations out of which, till then, they found no way to escape. They were built up in our most holy faith. They rejoiced in the Lord more abundantly. They were strengthened in love, and more effectually provoked to abound in every good work."[6]

Public confession of this kind continues to be a mark of the contemporary East African revival. The "fellowship meetings" of the "Balokole" or "saved ones" usually follow an identical pattern, the time of corporate Bible study being preceded by singing, extempore prayer, and a period of confession with testimony. Canon Max Warren, in his *Revival: An Enquiry*,[7] points out that "one of the dominant impulses from which revival is born is a recovered awareness of 'the exceeding sinfulness of sin.'" However we would define "revival," it is or includes a supernatural awareness of the presence of God. This brings a conviction of sin, or "brokenness," which in its turn "produces an impulse to confession." A second emphasis in the East African revival is on fellowship, on "walking in the light" with God and with each other. Only sin breaks this fellowship, and if the fellowship is to be restored, the sin must be confessed. Canon Warren quotes a missionary who allowed herself to be drawn into the movement because to hold back was "to refuse to be identified with the fellowship of forgiven sinners." Third, it is important to know that, over the course of the last twenty-five years, the emphasis on confession seems to have yielded to an emphasis on testimony. It is not enough to confess sin; "What is also looked for," says Dr. Warren, "is testimony to release from sin, to victory over sin." And as experiences of the power of Jesus to save are shared, the fellowship meeting is interrupted by the singing of "tukutendereza" (Luganda for "we praise thee"), a chorus which praises God for the cleansing blood of Jesus, the Lamb of God and Savior of sinners. This is thoroughly biblical. It is the other kind of "confession" found in the Bible, confession of Christ rather than confession of sin, and is in some ways greater even than testimony to Christ, for "while witness is addressed to men, confession is addressed in the presence of men to God in a voluntary impulse of gratitude and praise."[8] We are back in the atmosphere of the Psalms, in which a song of praise is sung in the congregation for some mighty deliverance of God: "He reached down from on high and took hold of me; he drew me out of deep waters" (Ps 18:16); "This poor man called, and the LORD heard him; he saved him out of all his troubles" (Ps 34:6); "He lifted me out of the slimy pit, out of the mud and mire; he set my feet on a rock and gave me a firm place to stand. He put a new song in my mouth, a hymn of praise to our God" (Ps 40:2–3); "The cords of death entangled me, the anguish of the grave came over me; I was overcome by distress and sorrow. Then I called on the name of the LORD: LORD, save me! The LORD is gracious and righteous; our God is full of compassion. The LORD protects the unwary; when I was brought low, he saved me. Return to your rest, my soul, for the LORD has been good to you. For you,

LORD, have delivered me from death, my eyes from tears, my feet from stumbling" (Ps 116:3–8).

There seems, therefore, to be far more biblical warrant for this kind of public confession of the Lord, than there is of the public confession of sin. Canon Warren is right to place "a question-mark" against the practice of public confession of sin. "Long Christian experience suggests," he adds, "that exhibitionism, prurience, and superficiality lurk in the shadows of this particular discipline." The test must always be whether the church is edified by it (1 Cor 14:26). Confession of sin may sometimes be unedifying, unhelpful; but the confession of Christ and of his power to save can encourage the downcast soul and lift the drooping spirit, provoking others in the fellowship to love and to good works (Heb 10:24–25).

Certainly there is a place for the confession of infirmity leading to a request for prayer; and we are plainly commanded to "carry each other's burdens, and in this way you will fulfill the law of Christ" (Gal 6:2); but this is best done, as the context in Galatians implies, between individual believers who seek to get alongside one another in a time of need.

Open and Disciplinary Confession

The first two forms of "public confession" which we have been considering are, strictly speaking, not public confession at all. Let me explain why. To "confess" is "to admit or declare oneself guilty of what one is accused of,"[9] and therefore confession is rightly made to the person who has been offended and is in a position to accuse one. This is why "secret" confession is properly made to God alone, "private" confession to the particular individual against whom one has sinned, and "public" confession to the church in the case of some public offense against the church. What we have so far been discussing in this chapter is really the confession of

37

secret sins against God or of private sins against our fellow men, which for some reason may be publicly acknowledged. But in its true sense "public confession" can only be made to the community against whom the sins in question have been committed.

Such "public confession" is the public acknowledgment to the church of some public offense against the church, so that the offender may be publicly forgiven and restored by the church. Without it he should be and remain publicly excommunicated. The most notable example of this in the Old Testament is Achan, whose disobedience in hoarding some booty which God had commanded to be destroyed had brought military disaster to Israel before Ai. Joshua said to Achan: "My son, give glory to the LORD, the God of Israel, and honor him. Tell me what you have done; do not hide it from me" (Jo 7:19). Achan had sinned against the people as well as against the Lord. His sin had therefore to be publicly confessed and publicly punished. What Achan was to the new nation of Israel, Ananias and Sapphira were to the infant church of Christ. Their sin was an attempt to deceive the whole Christian community. It could no more be kept secret than Achan's. It was visited upon them by a dramatic judgment of God (Acts 5:1–11).

There were unusual, supernatural elements in both these events, and we need now to turn to the more normal administration of discipline to public offenders which was commanded by Jesus and practiced by the New Testament church. We have already considered our Lord's instruction (Mt 18:15–17) regarding a brother who sins against us, that we are to go and tell him his fault privately "just between the two of you." If he listens to us, Jesus said, we have "won" him. But if he does not listen to us, we are to go to him a second time, taking with us "one or two others," who are evidently in a position to confirm the fact of his offense, in order that "every matter may be established by the testimony of two or three witnesses." This was the requirement in the law courts of Israel (Nm 35:30; Dt 19:15); it was to be the same in the public discipline of the church of Christ. If the offender refuses to listen to the corroborating witnesses, he is to be given a third chance. "Tell it to the church," Jesus said, clearly meaning the whole local congregation. But "if he refuses to listen even to the church, treat him as you would a pagan or a tax collector" (Mt 18:17). That is to say, he is to be excluded from the Christian fellowship. And then our Lord adds the statement: "Truly I tell you, whatever you bind on earth will be bound in heaven, and whatever you loose on earth will be loosed in heaven" (Mt 18:18).

These words have been variously interpreted. The rabbis in the Mishnah used the metaphor of "binding" and "loosing" for "forbidding" and "permitting" certain practices, so that E. A. Litton explains it of "framing and abrogating ecclesiastical regulations."[10] The Reformers, as we shall see in the next chapter, usually assumed that the expression "binding and loosing" was the same as "retaining and remitting sins," and applied it to the public preaching of the gospel. But the context in which it is here found strongly suggests that Jesus had ecclesiastical discipline in mind. Thus Bishop Jewel gives this alternative interpretation of "loosing": that the "minister, when any have offended their brothers' minds with some great offence, or notable and open crime, whereby they have as it were banished and made themselves strangers from the common fellowship and from the body of Christ, then, after perfect amendment of such persons, doth reconcile them, and bring them home again, and restore them to the company and unity of the faithful."[11] Similarly, "we say that the power, as well of loosing as also of binding, standeth in God's word; and the exercise or execution of the same standeth either in preaching, or else in sentence of correction and ecclesiastical discipline."[12]

It is urged by some that these interpretations are mutually exclusive, and that "binding" and "loosing" must refer either to precepts (which are thereby forbidden or permitted) or to persons (who are thereby excommunicated or restored). We have seen above that proper arguments may be advanced in favor of either interpretation. It is not certain, however, that we are obliged to choose between these interpretations, since in the exercise of discipline they are inevitably combined. If the church has authority to remove an offender from its fellowship and to restore him, it must have authority to determine the grounds on which it will do so. It is by "binding" and "loosing" certain practices (declaring them lawful or unlawful) that the church can go on to "bind" those who disregard its teaching and "loose" those who obey it, or, having disregarded it, repent.

This is not to claim for the church an absolute or authoritarian rule, for the church's authority in both ethical instruction and ecclesiastical discipline is always secondary, being subordinate to the Word of God (Article XX). Although authority to "bind" and "loose" seems in Matthew 18:18 to have been extended by Jesus to each local church, it was first given to Peter and with him (we believe) to his fellow apostles (Mt 16:19). So the local church may only administer discipline by reference to, and in submission to, the moral teaching of the apostles.

We see in the epistles of the New Testament how this authority was exercised in the first days of the church's life. The incestuous offender at Corinth, whose sin was evidently not a single act but that he was actually "sleeping with his father's wife" (1 Cor 5:1), and had not repented, was to be "expelled" or "put out" of the fellowship (5:2, 13). Such excommunication is called a "delivery to Satan" both here (5:5 RSV) and in 1 Timothy 1:20, presumably because the church is the sphere of Christ's rule and outside the church is "the dominion of darkness" (see also Acts 26:18; Col 1:13). We cannot be certain whether the offender mentioned in 2 Corinthians 2:5–11 is the same person, but in any case we are given there a complementary example of the forgiveness and restoration of a sinner who has been publicly punished. It is plain that during the period of excommunication, until and unless the offender has repented, confessed, and been restored, he is to be repudiated from fellowship. The

Christians were not even to associate with him (1 Cor 5:9–11;[13] see also Ti 3:10–11).

It is important to notice the cause and the purposes of this drastic discipline. The cause was in each case serious sin willfully persisted in. The list of grave moral offences which is given in 1 Corinthians 5:9–11 refers not to an isolated lapse, but to people whose lives are characterized and contaminated by immorality, idolatry, drunkenness, or greed. Similarly, it is only after admonishing a factious person once or twice (Ti 3:10), if he stubbornly refuses to obey apostolic teaching (2 Thes 3:14), and resists even the increasingly solemn rebukes prescribed by Jesus (Mt 18:15–17), that he is to be thus rejected.

The purposes of excommunication are retributive, remedial, and deterrent. All three are implied in the passages we have considered. The biblical writers do not shy away from the concept of retribution, as many modern thinkers do. The apostle Paul could write of "judging" and of "punishing" an offender (1 Cor 5:12–13; 2 Cor 2:6). He clearly regarded it as right and just that an open offender should be openly punished. Nevertheless, the discipline which punished him was intended, where possible, to reform him too. The obstinately disobedient brother was to be shunned "that he may feel ashamed" (2 Thes 3:14). Hymenaeus and Alexander were "handed over to Satan, to be taught not to blaspheme" (1 Tm 1:20). Even if the incestuous offender of Corinth was not restored, either on the occasion described in 2 Corinthians 2 or at any other time, the purpose of his excommunication was positive. It was "for the destruction of the flesh, that his spirit may be saved on the day of the Lord" (1 Cor 5:5). The destruction of his flesh might mean his sanctification, and certainly the Reformers constantly stressed that ecclesiastical discipline was intended to help an offender "to tame the flesh," but it probably refers to his physical death. In this case, even if he died for his sin, as did Ananias and Sapphira, and also other Corinthian Christians (1 Cor 11:30), the purpose of the excommunication was his final salvation. The third purpose was deterrent. Paul instructed Timothy to administer a public rebuke to "those who sin . . . , so that the others may take warning" (1 Tm 5:20).

This administration of church discipline was continued in the primitive church of the first few centuries. The commination service begins, as we have seen in an earlier chapter, with the statement that in those days "there was a godly discipline" by which "such persons as stood convicted of notorious sin were put to open penance, and punished in this world, that their souls might be saved in the day of the Lord; and that others, admonished by their example, might be the more afraid to offend." Precisely how it fell into desuetude is not known. It may be that during the fierce persecutions of the third century the discipline administered to those who lapsed was too severe, or, as Hooker suggests, that the scandal of public confessions became worse than the scandal of the sins themselves. But, whatever the cause, we know that this healthy and biblical practice of public confession and public penance became gradually displaced by the unhealthy and unbiblical practice of auricular confession and private penance. In the fifth century Pope Leo the Great wrote to the bishops of Campania that public confessions should no longer be made to the congregation but to the priest as their (N.B. not God's) representative. This practice seems to have become general by the end of the following century.

The Reformers were anxious to restore public discipline for serious offences. When preaching before King Henry VIII, Hugh Latimer, oppressed by the moral laxity of the country, appealed to him "to restore the discipline of Christ, and return to the church the power of excommunication."[14] The commination service, which is a general "denouncing of God's anger and judgments" against impenitent sinners, was offered as a substitute "until the said discipline may be restored again (which is much to be wished)." Meanwhile, one of the rubrics before the Holy Communion service instructs the minister to warn any "open and notorious evil liver," who has offended the congregation by word or deed, not to "presume . . . to come to the Lord's Table, until he have openly declared himself to have truly repented and amended his former naughty life, that the congregation may thereby be satisfied, which before were offended." So convinced were our Reformers of the necessity of this exercise of discipline, that it was sometimes added to the preaching of the pure Word of God and the due administration of the sacraments as a third mark of the visible church of Christ. Thus, in the second part of the Homily for Whitsunday, one of the "three notes or marks" of the church "whereby it is known" is "the right use of ecclesiastical discipline."[15] Although this phrase does not occur in Article XIX, Article XXXIII teaches with great definiteness that any person who "by open denunciation of the church is rightly cut off from the unity of the church and excommunicated" is to be treated by the multitude, as our Lord commanded, like "an heathen and publican, until he be openly reconciled by penance."

We today should share the desire of the Reformers for a restoration of this "godly discipline," in obedience to the plain instructions of our Lord and his apostles. The church's great weakness and ineffectiveness in our generation are undoubtedly due in part to its lack of discipline, not only in the administration of baptism and the Lord's Supper, but in the treatment of open offenders. At present the divorcee is commonly the only person who is excommunicated. This not only gives an exaggerated prominence to divorce, but appears to minimize the gravity of other offenses.[16] Of course there are many reasons advanced against the enforcement of a stricter discipline. The modern quest for the unity of the church; the hatred of all intolerance (which fails to distinguish between a right intolerance of sin and a wrong intolerance of spirit); a mistaken notion that such public discipline betokens pride, animosity, or priggishness; a horror of anything approaching the public accusation meetings promoted by Communist governments; a misinterpretation of the parable of the wheat and tares as prohibiting all attempts to separate the bad from the good in the visible church; a fear of public scandal in these days of mass media of communication—these and other arguments are used to hinder the restoration of a proper discipline to the church.

Let us agree that some of these arguments are not without substance, that the practice of ecclesiastical discipline is exposed to many perils, and that after many years of neglect great courage and wisdom will be needed to recover it. But the arguments in its favor are stronger and more compelling than the arguments against it. The eternal good of serious offenders is not served by lax discipline; we have seen that public discipline and excommunication in the New Testament were exercised for the reform and benefit of sinners. Again, the church's witness is impaired by its own low standards. The secular world is almost wholly unimpressed by the church today. There is a widespread departure from Christian moral standards, and unbelievers see no great difference between themselves and church members. So long as the church tolerates sin in itself and does not judge itself (1 Cor 5:12–13; 11:31; 1 Pt 4:17), and fails to manifest visibly the power of Jesus Christ to save from sin, it will never attract the world to Christ. And have we no vision of the purpose of Christ for his church, that we are content with our easy-going mediocrity? Jesus Christ "gave himself for us to redeem us from all wickedness and to purify for himself a people that are his very own, eager to do what is good" (Ti 2:14). He came from heaven to seek her as his bride. He "gave himself up for her to make her holy, cleansing her by the washing with water through the word, and to present her to himself as a radiant church, without stain or wrinkle or any other blemish, but holy and blameless" (Eph 5:25–27). How can we, in the light of this purpose of his death, remain indifferent to the church's holiness?

One last practical point. In the administration of discipline, the responsibility belongs to the whole local congregation. The power of the keys may have been given to Peter according to Matthew 16:19, although Bishop Jewel quoted Augustine in his

Defence of the Apology that "when Christ said unto Peter 'unto thee will I give the keys of the kingdom of heaven' he signified thereby the whole church."[17] At all events, a little later, this very same authority to bind and loose was explicitly granted by Jesus to each local church, according to Matthew 18:17–18. "Tell it to the church," he had just said. It is true that the apostle Paul, when instructing the Corinthian church what they must do, indicated that his spirit would be present with them while they did it, but still it was *they* who, with the power of the Lord Jesus, were to "hand over to Satan" the offender, and "expel" him out from their fellowship (1 Cor 5). Of course the local church should only act in agreement with its pastor, and will in any case act through its pastor, and the pastor should consult his bishop, but biblical discipline is essentially parochial and not diocesan, congregational and not ministerial or episcopal. It is the local church which has been sinned against; it is the local church to which public confession must be made; and it is the local church which must take responsibility to administer discipline and to use its God-given authority to bind and to loose.

CHAPTER FOUR

Auricular Confession 1 (to a priest)

The Minister's Authority

It was suggested in the Introduction that the existence of an in-dissoluble link between sin, confession, and forgiveness is com-mon ground between Christians of all persuasions. We are all agreed that in order to receive the forgiveness of sin the confes-sion of sin is indispensable. In answer to the question "to whom should we confess our sins," the Bible has been seen to teach that secret sins should be confessed secretly (to God), private sins privately (to a fellow human being we have wronged), and public sins publicly (to the local church). We are now in a posi-tion to ask the further, specific question: can any place be found in this biblical scheme for the practice of "auricular confession," confession *ad auriculam*, "into the ear" of a priest, or what the Reformers sometimes termed "earish" confession? We have already seen that it developed gradually from the wholesome discipline of open confession and open penance, and that the Lateran Council of 1215 under Pope Innocent III made it com-pulsory for every Christian at least once a year. We no doubt also know that weekly confession is practiced by Roman Catholics today, and that since the Tractarian Movement at the beginning of the last century, weekly or less regular confession has become widespread among Anglo-Catholic churchmen in the Anglican Communion. Further, it is not uncommon nowadays for the practice to be commended by Anglicans who would not welcome the label "Anglo-Catholic."

Let me say at once that, from the purely historical point of view, leaving aside for the moment the question of biblical warrant, neither the custom of the primitive church nor the formularies of the Church of England support or encourage the practice as a normal, regular, or healthy part of the Christian life. Some students of early church history have been too ready to find in any patristic mention of "confession" an allusion to auricular confession to a priest. Bishop John Jewel did not hesitate to write that "the express term of auricular or secret confession is never mentioned in the ancient fathers."[1] Richard Hooker went further. He described how what they called "private penitency" had come to be regarded as "a sacrament of remitting sins after baptism," and a little later wrote: "I dare boldly affirm, that for many hundred years after Christ the fathers held no such opinion; they did not gather by our Saviour's words any such necessity of seeking the priest's absolution from sin, by secret and (as they now term it) sacramental confession." Was this custom not primitive then? "No, no," Hooker replies, "these opinions have youth in their countenance; antiquity knew them not: it never thought nor dreamed of them."[2] Thus, the author of the homily *Of Repentance* quotes St. Augustine's words: "What have I to do with men, that they should hear my confession, as though they were able to heal all my diseases?"[3] And Frederick Meyrick, himself an old-fashioned high churchman, collected a number of quotations from the sermons of St. Chrysostom and from his *De Poenitentia* in which sinners are urged not to uncover their sins to men, their "fellow servants," but in secret, "no one being present except the all-seeing God."[4]

It is quite true that, in the earlier years of the sixteenth century, before the Reformation had reached its zenith, our Anglican divines still commended auricular confession. In the eighth article of the Thirteen Articles of 1538, for instance, it is described as "very useful and highly necessary," although even then Cranmer would have preferred "convenient" to "necessary" and wanted to add that it was "not enjoined in Scripture." The Six Articles of the following year, known as "the whip with six strings" because by it Henry VIII tried to enforce uniformity of doctrine by the threat of severe penalties, affirmed that auricular confession was "necessary to be retained and continued, used and frequented in the Church of God."

The famous *King's Book* of 1543 (The Necessary Doctrine and Erudition of a Christian Man), which belonged to the twilight stage of the Reformation, called the sacrament of penance "the ordinary mean for penitent sinners to obtain remission of sins," and Cranmer's catechism of 1548 similarly called it a "sacrament" and the way to receive the forgiveness of sins committed after baptism. The same year (1548), however, in his Order of the Holy Communion, the first communion service to be written and published in the English language, the first exhortation referred to "a general confession" and "the auricular and secret confession to a priest" as alternatives, and urged the champions of the one not to be offended by the champions of the other, but to follow their own conscience and live in charity. This was incorporated in the first Reformed Prayer Book which appeared the following year.[5] But in the second Prayer Book of 1552 the wording of the first exhortation was changed to make secret confession to God the ordinary means of preparing to come to the Lord's Table, while the private resort to a "discreet and learned minister of God's Word" (which was not now called "auricular and secret confession to a priest") was relegated to the exceptional case of a person "who by this means cannot quiet his own conscience." It is in this sense that Ridley, Latimer, Becon, Tyndale, and other Reformers mention it appreciatively, as an abnormal but legitimate means of relieving a troubled conscience, not because they believed in the necessity of regular priestly absolution; and it is in this sense that it is still permitted in the Prayer Book of 1662.

But why is the regular use of auricular confession to be deprecated? I am not going to use or elaborate any of those popular arguments which have been based on the abuse of the confessional; right-minded "Catholics" deplore these things as much as any evangelical. Nor am I concerned so much with what greatly bothered the Reformers, namely, in words taken from the *Second Book of Homilies*, that "it is against the true Christian liberty that any man should be bound to the numbering of his sins."[6] Nor shall we spend time discussing the potential danger of this practice to the soul of the priest who hears confessions, although I must agree with Bishop J. C. Ryle that he is in "a place which it is not safe for any child of Adam to occupy."[7] If we are to "[hate] even the clothing stained by corrupted flesh" (Jude 23), like people afraid of a contagious disease, and if "it is shameful even to mention what the disobedient do in secret" (Eph 5:12), it seems to me very doubtful if God ever meant his ministers to have to enter thus into the secret sins of others. Nevertheless, it is neither because of the abuse, nor because of the perils, of auricular confession that I believe it should be avoided by those who do not use it, and abandoned by those who do, but because the very practice itself is misconceived. I submit that this form of confession is not the will and purpose of God either for the penitent who confesses or for the priest who absolves.

Yet it is precisely this which those who commend the practice claim. Their major arguments are first that it is a right and proper thing in itself, that it is in fact the plan of God that the priest should absolve the penitent in this way; and secondly that it is expedient, being of great practical benefit to the penitent in his spiritual pilgrimage. We shall consider the theological argument in this chapter, and the practical argument in the next. In this way we shall be able to consider both Christian ministers and the nature of their ministerial authority, and also Christian people and the means of their spiritual growth.

The "Catholic" View

The medieval schoolmen, like Duns Scotus, taught quite plainly that Christ had given the keys of the kingdom to priests, and that therefore heaven could be opened or closed to men at the sentence of a catholic priest alone. More precisely, original and pre-baptismal sins were put away by baptism, venial sins after baptism by penitence and the mass, and mortal sins after baptism by the sacrament of penance, although only partially. The Council of Trent, in Sessions XIII and XIV, made the sacrament of penance, including auricular confession, a necessary condition of coming to the Eucharist, and anathematized those who denied either its divine origin or its necessity for salvation. It was to be a regular practice binding on all Catholics. According to Cardinal Bellarmine, the sixteenth-century Jesuit who sought to defend Rome against the Reformers, Christ had "ordained His priests judges in such sort that no man which sinneth after baptism can be reconciled unto God but by their sentence."[8]

This is still the official teaching of the Roman Catholic Church, which (it is important to grasp) rests on their doctrine of the priesthood. Their view of confession arises from and depends on their view of absolution. According to Ludwig Ott's book *Fundamentals of Catholic Dogma*, the argument runs like this: when Jesus was on earth he forgave sins (Mk 2:5; Lk 7:47).[9] This very same power to forgive sins he bestowed "on the Apostles and on their legitimate successors"[10] who are not "all the faithful indiscriminately, but only . . . the members of the hierarchy"[11]— that is, catholic priests. He promised it to them in his words about the keys of the kingdom and about binding and loosing, both of which include "the power to forgive sins," and then actually transferred it to them "on the evening of the day of the Resurrection," when he said to them "As the Father hath sent me, I also send you . . . ; whose sins you shall forgive, they are forgiven them; and whose sins you shall retain, they are retained."[12] This "power to forgive sins involves not merely the power of preaching the gospel of the forgiveness of sins, as the Reformers interpreted it, but also the full power of really remitting sins."[13] Again, "the Church firmly insists that the power of absolution is a true and real power of absolution, by which sins committed against God are immediately remitted. The proof derives from John 20:23. According to the words of Jesus, the act of the remission of sins, performed by the apostles and by their successors, has the effect that sins are remitted by God. There is a causal connection between the active remitting and the passive being remitted."[14] Priestly absolution "does not merely indicate forgiveness of sins, but also effects it."[15]

Moreover, "the priestly absolution is a judicial act."[16] As such, it includes "three essential elements, (*a*) judicial power (*auctoritas iudicalis*), (*b*) knowledge of the state of the facts (*cognitio causae*) and (*c*) judicial sentence (*sententia iudicalis*)"[17] The second of these three is necessary because the judicial sentence imposed by the judicial authority would be arbitrary if it were not "related to . . . the state of conscience of the sinner." The sentence must be based on a knowledge of the facts and therefore presupposes an "investigation of the guilt and disposition of the sinner."[18] We must notice the roundabout way in which the subject of confession is reached. It is conceded that "the Divine institution and the necessity for salvation of the particular confession of sins is not explicitly expressed in Holy Writ"; nevertheless "it is a necessary consequence of the judicial power to forgive sins. The power of remitting sins or of retaining them can only be properly exercised, if the possessor of the power of penance knows both the sins and the dispositions of the penitent. But the self-accusation of the penitent is necessary for this." So comes the definition of confession as "the self-accusation by the penitent of his sins before a fully-empowered priest, in order to obtain forgiveness from him by virtue of the power of the keys." Therefore "the sacramental confession of sins is ordained of God and is necessary for salvation."[19]

What emerges from this account of the official teaching of

the Church of Rome is that its practice of auricular confession is grounded upon its doctrine of the priesthood and its unique authority to absolve from sin. If their foundation doctrine can be shown to be faulty, the confessional (at least as they describe it) will be discredited also. It is quite true that Anglican writers who commend the practice of auricular confession do not usually base their arguments on a fully developed "catholic" doctrine of priesthood. They tend to argue their case rather from the pragmatic benefits of confession than from a doctrinaire view of absolution. Yet their position still derives from John 20:23. Lord Halifax, at the Fulham Conference in December 1901, could go so far as to state "that the act of absolution is not merely declaratory, but is instrumental in conveying forgiveness."[20] He later added that "people do not go to confession to relieve their minds, or primarily for advice, but to get absolution for their sins in the way our Lord has appointed."[21] Manasses in his little book entitled *Go in Peace* writes that "we come to the priest in confession for absolution," and although he adds that this is "to receive God's forgiveness of our sins," he does not shrink from expressions like "he will then give you absolution" and "we do receive absolution and that is the greatest of gifts in this sacrament."[22] Similarly Wilfred Knox can write that "the words of absolution have bestowed on him for his particular sins that pardon which was won for all mankind once and for all by the death of Jesus on the Cross," although he adds that the priest is "the medium of a divine gift, not the bestower of it."[23] Again, the Rev. Kenneth Ross, in his *Instruction on Confession* which he has kindly allowed me to see, begins "(1) Jesus forgave sins . . . (2) Jesus passed on the power specifically: John 20:21–23." He thus assumes that the two activities are identical, before he goes on to suggest that the power was exercised first through baptism and ecclesiastical discipline, and now through private confession and absolution. From these quotations it seems fair to say that, although Anglo-Catholic writers do not define the authority of priestly absolution with the precision of Roman Catholics, or make confession compulsory as "necessary to salvation," they still regard absolution as the foremost benefit of confession and believe that the priest has unique power to "give" it to the penitent. They would agree that auricular confession is, strictly, not *to* a priest, but "the confession of sins to God in the presence of a priest authorized to forgive them in His name" (*Oxford Dictionary of the Christian Church*). The fundamental question remains: What is the nature of this authority?

The Biblical Teaching

We have already noted that there are three sayings of Jesus on which the claim to a unique priestly authority to absolve is based. They concern three pairs of activities, stated positively and negatively: to lock and to unlock (implied by the gift of "the keys of the kingdom of heaven," Mt 16:19), to bind and to loose (Mt 16:19; 18:18), to remit and to retain sins (Jn 20:23). The Reformers did not dispute the Roman Catholic view that the first two pairs were a metaphorical description of the third, that what was promised in Matthew 16 and 18 was actually given in John 20, or that all three passages referred to a certain authority in connection with forgiveness and the withholding of forgiveness. They maintained, however, that this authority lay not in the priesthood but in the gospel, not in the words of men but in the Word of God. The key which Jesus gave to his church was "nothing else but the holy Word of God," wrote Robert Barnes, "this is the thing only whereby that our conscience is loosed and made free from sin."[24] Possessing this key the apostles "did bind with the Word when it was not believed; they did loose by the Word when it was believed: thus did they by one Word preach both salvation and damnation." Becon put the same conviction in very similar terms, that Christian preachers of the Word of God "loosen, that is to say, they preach to the faithful remission of sins by Christ. They also bind, that is, they declare to the unfaithful damnation."[25] Even more explicitly, William Tyndale wrote: "To bind and to loose is to preach the law of God and the Gospel or promises, as thou mayest see in the third chapter of the second epistle to the Corinthians, where Paul calleth the preaching of the law the ministration of death and damnation, and the preaching of the promises the ministering of the Spirit and of righteousness."[26] Jewel explained in *The Apology* how the minister "looses" when he offers "by the preaching of the Gospel the merits of Christ and full pardon to such as have lowly and contrite hearts and do unfeignedly repent them, pronouncing unto the same a sure and undoubted forgiveness of their sins and hope of everlasting salvation," and "binds" when he "shutteth up the gate of the kingdom of heaven against the unbelieving and stubborn persons, denouncing unto them God's vengeance and everlasting punishment."[27] In *The Defence of the Apology*, Jewel supported his interpretation of the keys from the fathers: "We with Chrysostom say 'they be the knowledge of the Scriptures,' with Tertullian we say, 'they be the interpretation of the Law,' and with Eusebius we call them 'the Word of God.'"[28]

It must be admitted that the Reformers were a little uncritical in assuming that locking and unlocking with the keys, binding and loosing, and remitting and retaining sins were simple synonyms. Let us consider them separately. We cannot deny that the keys were given to Simon Peter personally. Unlike the scribes and Pharisees who had "taken away the key to knowledge" (Lk 11:52) and "shut the door of the kingdom of heaven in people's faces" (Mt 23:13), Peter was to use the keys to open it, and he did so first to the Jews (Acts 2:38), secondly to the Samaritans (Acts 8:14-16), and then to the Gentiles (Acts 10-11; see also 15:7). The unique privilege which the keys brought him was one of historical priority in opening the kingdom, not of permanent primacy.

Immediately after promising to give Peter "the keys of the kingdom of heaven," Jesus went on to say to him: "whatever you bind on earth will be bound in heaven, and whatever you loose on earth will be loosed in heaven" (Mt 16:19). He later extended this authority to each local church (Mt 18:17–18). The use of the neuter "whatever" (which seems to refer to things, not people) and the rabbinic use of the metaphor for permissions and prohibitions in the realm of conduct,[29] tend to confirm Bishop John Wordsworth's opinion that "on this text we may rest the validity of the canonical rules of the church, but not the ministry of penitence to persons."[30] Further, as was indicated in the last chapter, the context in Matthew 18 suggests that ecclesiastical discipline was in our Lord's mind, namely the further authority to excommunicate an offender and to restore him when he repented. Hooker took it thus: "The Church bindeth by the censures of her discipline" and "the Church looseth but her own bands, the chains wherein she had tied them before."[31] In this sense the church has an authority to grant an absolute forgiveness to those who have offended against her; she has no such authority to forgive those who have offended against God.

If the power of the keys and the activity of binding and loosing do not necessarily refer to the forgiveness of sins against God, the direct statement in John 20:23 about "forgiving" and "not forgiving" sins clearly does. Two questions confront us. First, to whom was this authority given? Secondly, of what did the authority consist? It is an essential part of the Roman Catholic system that the power of absolution was given only to the apostles and their successors, the priests. This cannot be proved. Quite apart from the lack of any reference to the transmission of the authority, and of any identification of those to whom it might be transmitted, and of any suggestion in the New Testament that there is a priestly or sacerdotal ministry in the Christian church[32] or that "absolution" is necessarily a function of "priests," there is no evidence that the words of the risen Jesus recorded in John 20:23 were spoken to the apostles alone. Was the Great Commission, sending them into the world as the Father had sent him, addressed to the apostles only? Was the Holy Spirit, whose Pentecostal coming he anticipated by breathing on them in a dramatic acted parable, to be given to the apostles alone? If we are not prepared to restrict to the apostles our Lord's sending of them out or giving to them the Spirit, we cannot properly restrict his promise about remitting and retaining sins to the apostles either. Besides, if we insist that the power to absolve was given to all the apostles and to them alone, it will have included Thomas although he was absent (Jn 20:24), yet excluded the Emmaus disciples and others, although they were present (Lk 24:33). There is no indication that Jesus discriminated like this. We must therefore conclude that the bestowal of authority, like the Great Commission and the promise of the Spirit, was made indiscriminately to all present as the nucleus of the whole church.

What, then, was this authority? It is *a priori* improbable that Jesus was actually transferring to the church the same authority to forgive sins which he had claimed and exercised himself (Mk 2:7). His hearers understandably accused him of blasphemy, since they recognized that to forgive sins is a divine prerogative. Besides, he claimed that he had this authority as "the Son of Man" (his favorite Messianic title), just as in the other controversy stories in this chapter of St. Mark he defended his actions by claiming to be the Good Physician of sinners, the heavenly Bridegroom and the Lord of the Sabbath (Mk 2:17, 19, 28). Are we proposing to transfer these offices to the church as well? No, these titles and the functions which go with them belong exclusively to Jesus because of who he was and is. We cannot forgive sins as he did for we are not the Son of Man, any more than we are the sinners' Physician, the church's Bridegroom, or the Sabbath's Lord. This being so, we must interpret his description of the church "forgiving" and "not forgiving" people's sins as a dramatic figure of speech for a dogmatic declaration in certain circumstances that their sins are forgiven or not forgiven. This would be in keeping with other startling expressions of Jesus like "hating" our parents, "plucking out" our eyes, "taking up our cross," and "losing our life." The interpretation of the verbs "forgiving" and "not forgiving" as the verbal declaration of a truth is paralleled in the publicans' "justifying God" (Lk 7:29; so Hooker) and in Jeremiah's "destroying" and "building up" the nation of Judah which, Tyndale argued, was "verily by preaching and prophesying."[33]

If it be asked by what principles we thus interpret this controversial verse, we must reply: by the two most important and reliable of all the canons of biblical interpretation, namely the comparison of parallel passages and the understanding of the original hearers. If we compare Scripture with Scripture, and especially the wording of the Great Commission as it is recorded here in St. John and in St. Luke 24:46–49, we find similar references to the evangelization of the world, the gift of the Spirit, and the offer of forgiveness. But the "forgiveness of sins" which in St. John is portrayed as an activity of the disciples in St. Luke is the substance of the message which they are to preach in his Name among all nations (Lk 24:47). The natural explanation of the parallel is that the Johannine statement is a strikingly forceful version of the Lucan, and is to be interpreted in the same way, as a proclamation.

The second principle of exegesis concerns the understanding of the original hearers. We must always beware of imposing upon Scripture the ideas of a later age. The fatal objection to the "catholic" explanation of John 20:23 as the bestowal of a judicial, absolving authority is that the apostles never spoke or behaved as if they understood it in this way. There is no evidence in the New Testament that they believed such an authority had been given them. They neither claimed these powers, nor exercised them. What they did, on the other hand, was to declare with authority the terms on which God would forgive men's sins through Christ, and then to admit penitent believers by baptism into the church (Acts 2:38; 3:19; 13:38–39; 22:16; 26:17–18, etc.). Similarly, in the epistles, even in the pastoral epistles, there are no verses which can be construed as an allusion to private confession and absolution, but only triumphant affirmations that "in [Christ] we have redemption through his blood, the forgiveness of sins" (Eph 1:7; Col

1:14). Paul understood the "ministry of reconciliation" committed to the church as a proclamation of "the message of reconciliation" and an appeal, as Christ's ambassadors, to men to be reconciled to God (2 Cor 5:18-21). As Becon put it: "Neither did the apostles absolve any otherwise than by the preaching of God's Word."[34]

From these biblical data we conclude that the authority to "forgive" and "not forgive" sins, which the risen Christ gave to his disciples, was ministerial, not magisterial. It was not an authority to forgive, but to preach forgiveness, to proclaim "not simply with words but also with power, with the Holy Spirit and deep conviction" (1 Thes 1:5) both the promises and the warnings of the gospel—the promise of salvation to the believer, the warning of judgment to the unbeliever. Moreover, this authority was given by Christ to the whole church, to whom the universal commission and the gift of the Spirit were also given. As Bishop Jewel wrote: "Christ's disciples did receive this authority, not that they should hear the private confessions of the people . . ., but to the end they should go, they should teach, they should publish abroad the Gospel."[35] True, it is an authority exercised primarily through ministers duly called and ordained to preach the Word, but this limitation is one of expediency rather than of necessity. It is God who forgives through Christ; it is the church which proclaims his forgiveness through its ministers.

The Prayer Book

But, it may be asked, is this interpretation, of an authority to declare sins remitted or retained, delegated to ministers by the church, consistent with the prayer books of the Anglican Communion? In particular, is it not contradicted by the authority ascribed to ministers in the Ordinal, the first exhortation of the communion service, and the Visitation of the Sick in the 1662 book? Do they not imply that the priest has the power by virtue of his ordination to absolve sins? These questions are often asked and must be plainly answered. Moreover, in answering them we must be careful not to offer an explanation which is incompatible either with the Prayer Book as a whole or with the known opinions of our Reformers as disclosed in their writings, the Articles, and Homilies. We must give them credit for logical and consistent thought and not impute to them either confused minds or self-contradictory utterances.

The actual words spoken by the bishop while hands are being laid on the candidate for full orders are in three parts. First: "Receive the Holy Ghost for the office and work of a priest in the Church of God, now committed unto thee by the imposition of our hands." The word "priest" is unfortunately ambiguous in modern ears, but not in the writings of the Reformers. It is an English contraction of the word "presbyter," and refers not to distinctively sacerdotal functions in the ministry, which the Reformers had abandoned, but to the second of the three orders, "bishops, priests (that is, presbyters) and deacons" (see the Preface to the Ordinal). Secondly, the words of Jesus are quoted: "Whose sins thou dost forgive, they are forgiven; and whose sins thou dost retain, they are retained." These words had appeared in unreformed ordinals from the thirteenth century, but not in association with the act of ordination itself. Cranmer took them "out of a subordinate position, and made them the actual formula of ordination."[36] How he intended them to be understood is made clear by the charge which immediately follows: "And be thou a faithful dispenser of the Word of God, and His holy sacraments." This is further emphasized by the *traditio instrumentorum* which comes next, while the candidate remains kneeling. He is not given a paten and chalice, with bread and wine, as in the medieval services, with the words, "Receive power to offer sacrifice to God, and to celebrate Masses for the living and for the dead," nor even a Bible in one hand and a chalice in the other (as in 1550), but a Bible only, with the words, "Take thou authority to preach the Word of God, and to minister the holy sacraments in the congregation." It is this emphasis on the Word of God, in the ministry of preaching and the sacraments alike, which interprets the meaning of John 20:23 in this context. "If we can only get back," wrote Bishop Drury, "to the original breadth of that solemn commission, and read those words . . . in the large sense that the Reformers attached to them, we need not regret that our Church, in granting her commission, uses the *ipsissima verba* with which she received it."[37] They indicate in graphic terms both the substance of the church's message and the authority with which it is to be proclaimed.

Turning from the Ordinal to the first exhortation of the communion service, the best way to discover what the Reformers intended by it is to compare the significant ways in which the wording of the 1549 Prayer Book was altered in that of 1552. Apart from the fact that a private resort to the minister, which in 1549 was a recognized alternative to general confession, has now become exceptional, there were two principal changes—regarding the character of the "confession" and the means of "absolution." In 1549 we still read of "the auricular and secret confession to a priest," and the invitation to the conscience-stricken penitent is: "Let him come to me or to some other discreet and learned priest taught in the law of God, and confess and open his sin and grief secretly." In 1552, however, the person who cannot quiet his conscience is not to confess his sin to a priest, but rather to "open his grief" to a "discreet and learned minister of God's word."[38] The absolution is different too. In both forms the penitent is to receive not only "counsel" and "advice," but absolution—in 1549 "of us (as ministers of God and of his church)," in 1552 "by the ministry of God's holy word." The authoritative message of assurance is to come not from the words of men but from the Word of God himself, as, in Girdlestone's rather quaint phrase, "whilst the inquirer opens his grief, the minister opens his Bible."[39] This interpretation of private "absolution" as authority through the ministry of God's Word to pronounce a penitent and believing sinner forgiven is consistent with the public absolutions at Morning and Evening Prayer and at Holy Communion. In the former services the absolution is plainly declaratory, the "power and commandment" which God has given to his ministers being "to declare and pronounce to His people, being penitent, the absolution and remission of their sins." They do not "give" absolution but proclaim it; the gift is God's, for "*He* pardoneth and absolveth all them that truly repent and unfeignedly believe His holy Gospel." The minister therefore concludes by exhorting the congregation to pray that God will give us (minister and people alike) "true repentance and His Holy Spirit," without which God's forgiveness cannot be received. In the Holy Communion service there is neither a "giving" of absolution, nor even a "declaration" of it, but a prayer for it, grounded upon God's merciful promise of "forgiveness of sins to all them that with hearty repentance and true faith turn unto Him." This reference to God's promise is immediately confirmed by the recitation of the four "Comfortable Words," which are gracious invitations and pledges of the gospel—"gospel-comfort" in fact, in the expression of Hermann's German liturgy. Thus again the pardon of man and the assurance of it flow from the Word of God.

A rubric in the Order for the Visitation of the Sick reads: *"Here shall the sick person be moved to make a special confession of his sins, if he feel his conscience troubled with any weighty matter. After which confession, the priest shall absolve him (if he humbly and heartily desire it) after this sort."* The first point to be noted here is that both the confession and the absolution are exceptional and voluntary. The two conditional "if" clauses show this. It is only if a sick person has some "weighty matter" on his conscience that he is to be "moved" (that is, encouraged, not commanded) to "make a special confession of his sins."[40] And it is only "if he humbly and heartily desire it" that the minister is to "absolve him." What form will this optional absolution take? No obligatory form is prescribed. The words which follow may be used either as a form or as a pattern ("after this sort"). They comprise two complementary parts. The first addresses Jesus Christ as the one who has left "power to His church" (not just his ministers) to absolve, not "all sinners," but all those "who truly repent and believe in Him," and prays that "of His great mercy" he will forgive the penitent's offenses. In the second part the minister says: "By His authority committed to me" (that is, delegated to me by the church to whom it was originally given) "I absolve thee from all thy sins, in the Name of the Father, and of the Son, and of the Holy Ghost. Amen."

This phrase has been taken by some to mean that the Church of England claims for its ministers the power of judicial absolution. Certainly the formula is the "catholic" one, *ego absolvo te*, but there is no justification for interpreting it in the "catholic" way. We have liberty to understand it only in the light of the known theological position of the Reformers. We must agree with the Puritans that it is ambiguous. At the Savoy Conference they wanted the formula changed from "I absolve thee" to "I pronounce thee absolved." But the bishops justly replied that the words were "more agreeable to the Scriptures than that which they desire," since they are an echo of John 20:23. We must balance the minister's statement of absolution with the prayer to God for it which both precedes and follows, and we must understand the statement itself as the Reformers did.[41] Hugh Latimer in a famous sermon on the petition for forgiveness in the Lord's Prayer, preached in 1552, claimed that "a godly minister . . . instructed in the Word of God" could absolve sinners "in open preaching" and went on to explain what he meant: "As many as confess their sins unto God, acknowledging themselves to be sinners, and believe that our Saviour, through His passion, hath taken away their sins, and have an earnest purpose to leave sin, as many I say as be so affectioned, *ego absolvo vos*: I, as an officer of Christ, as His treasurer, absolve you in His name. This is the absolution that I can make by God's Word."[42] The absolution in the Visitation of the Sick is simply a personal and particular application of this general authoritative ministry of the Word. Thus Bishop Christopher Wordsworth of Lincoln wrote in a pastoral letter dated 1874, and quoted by Bishop Drury: "By those words 'I absolve,' we do not claim for ourselves the power to give pardon, but only as heralds sent from God Himself, to certify and assure you, that He is ever ready to be gracious . . . and that if you have true repentance, lively faith, and fervent love . . . He has washed away your sins in the Blood of Christ, and will remember them no more."[43]

With this position, of course, the formularies of the other Reformed churches of the sixteenth century are in complete agreement. To take one example, chapter 14 of the Second Helvetic Confession speaks as follows:

> All ministers, truly called, have and exercise the keys, or the use of them, when they preach the Gospel, that is to say, when they teach, exhort, reprove, and keep in order the people committed to their charge. It is thus that they open the kingdom of God to the obedient and shut it against the disobedient . . . Rightly, therefore, and effectually do ministers absolve. when they preach the Gospel of Christ, and thereby remission of sins, which is promised to everyone that believes. . . . Nor do we imagine that this absolution is in the slightest degree more effectual by being mumbled privately into some priest's ear or over some man's head; yet we judge that men must be taught diligently to seek remission of sins in the blood of Christ and that all should be reminded that forgiveness of sins belongs to Him alone.

God's way of forgiveness according to the Scriptures is plain. The authority to forgive sins he has given to Jesus Christ his Son alone, who died for our sins and whose blood of the New Covenant was shed for the forgiveness of sins. The authority which Jesus Christ has given to his church, and which the church delegates largely (but not entirely) to its ministers, is to preach the gospel of forgiveness in his Name (Lk 24:47; Acts 13:38–39), and to declare with confident authority to those who repent and believe that their sins are indeed forgiven. We cannot avoid the conclusion that to go to a human priest privately, to confess our sins and to seek absolution, is not the way which God has appointed. The Christian ministry resembles that of John the Baptist. It is a signpost ministry pointing to Christ. Our constant theme must be: "Behold the Lamb of God." We do not, therefore, say to sinners "Come to me" (except in exceptional cases which we shall consider in the next chapter), for those are the words of Christ. What we say is "Go to him." The habitual practice of auricular confession is damaging to the penitent (since it at least confuses, if not contradicts, his God-given right of direct access to Jesus Christ); it is falsely glorifying to the minister (since it implies a judicial authority to forgive which he does not possess); and it is derogatory to Jesus Christ (since it obscures his uniqueness as our only and absolutely adequate Savior, Mediator, and Advocate: 1 Tm 2:5; 1 Jn 2:1-2). Bishop Ryle was right to ask what the sense or reason was of going to an earthly confessor so long as we can have access to the best of all Priests, Jesus Christ himself: "When His ear is deaf, and His heart is cold—when His hand is feeble, and His power to heal is exhausted—when the treasure-house of His sympathy is empty, and His love and goodwill have become cold—then and not till then, it will be time to turn to earthly priests and earthly confessionals. Thank God, that time is not yet come!"[44]

CHAPTER FIVE

Auricular Confession 2 (to a priest)

The Penitent's Need

The two principal arguments by which the practice of auricular confession has been commended are first theological, that God has willed it this way (giving his priests authority to absolve) and secondly practical, that sinners need it this way (it is most helpful and beneficial to us). The Reformers certainly agreed that, rightly understood and shorn of unbiblical notions of priesthood and absolution, it should be retained for *exceptional* cases. It is, as we have seen, in this sense that the references to it in the English Prayer Book are to be understood. But modern writers of varying schools of thought, though not wishing to make it compulsory, strongly urge that it should be *habitual*. They do not think of it "as a medicine for special cases of sickness" but "as food for the soul in ordinary health."[1] Thus, P. D. Butterfield commends "the practice of regular sacramental confession as one of proven usefulness in the Christian life."[2] To Wilfred Knox "the value of the Sacrament of Penance cannot be overestimated."[3] Eric James writes of his conviction that "everything possible must be done to proclaim that the sacrament of Confession is available for all in the Church of England."[4]

I must honestly say that these and other modern writers seem to me to rely too much on arguments of expediency. We are all agreed about our human degradation, our sin and guilt, our way-

65

wardness and weakness. We know that "there is no health in us." So what do we do? Well, we are too precipitate in prescribing the remedy which *we* favor, instead of consulting the Great Physician and applying the remedies which he prescribes. After all, the first criterion by which a Christian judges a course of action is not its apparent value, but its rightness. The first question we should ask about any practice is not "is it useful?" but "is it biblical?" Is it part of the gracious revealed purpose of our Savior for the salvation and sanctification of sinners? If not, then what *is* his purpose for them? I find it alarming that so few modern writers seem to stop to ask these questions and to get a satisfactory answer to them. It is this failure to begin from first principles which has led many to adopt and commend a practice which, although undoubtedly helpful to some people in special need, is not for the highest good of the average Christian, because it is not God's normal purpose for him.

Perhaps the best way to proceed will be to consider the benefits which are claimed for the practice of regular confession, and then to examine if there is some other, better way by which these benefits may be secured. The forms of confession which I have seen put into the penitent's mouth, after the enumeration of his sins and the expression of his sorrow and resolve to amend, are requests for "penance, advice, and absolution." We could profitably take these requests as summarizing the value said to be derived from confession: "penance" to humble us and help us see the sinfulness of our sins; "absolution" to assure us of God's forgiveness; and "advice" to guide us in our Christian growth and discipline. These are certainly three great benefits. We all need to be convicted of the gravity of our sins, comforted by the forgiveness of our sins, and counselled about the conquest of our sins. The question is: What is the best and God-appointed means to secure these proper ends?

Repentance

According to Roman Catholic theologians, the outward signs of the sacrament of penance are said to be "contrition, confession, and satisfaction." "Contrition" is a grief and hatred of sin, with a resolve not to sin again, while "attrition" is the word they use for an imperfect contrition proceeding not from the love of God but from fear of punishment or other lesser motives. They further teach that one of the valuable effects of the sacrament of penance is that it turns attrition into contrition. Anglican theologians do not favor this kind of subtlety but do teach the value of confession to deepen the penitent's contrition, which is a necessary sign of his repentance and condition of his forgiveness (Ps 51:17; 2 Cor 7:10). No one will deny P. D. Butterfield's statement that God "calls us sooner or later to deepened penitence"; but I must question his conclusion that "for most of us, when we have put away prejudice and fear, that means going to confession."[5] I question this not because I doubt the costliness to human pride involved in the practice, but because I do not believe this is God's normal method of humbling and convicting the sinner.

Let us examine the arguments further. "The sorrow is increased by the use of sacramental confession," writes Manasses: "the fact of somebody else hearing what we have to say increases our horror at what we have done, and at what we have omitted to do."[6] Eric James suggests that as the prodigal son could have written his father a letter of apology but found "owning up to his face . . . more costly" and productive of a "deeper reconciliation," so in sacramental confession we can speak to God "face to face" more than when we are on our own. "This sacrament enables repentance to be increasingly deep," he writes later.[7] But it is Wilfred Knox who lays most emphasis on this point. He refers to it several times in his book *Penitence and Forgiveness*. He describes "the Sacrament of Penance as a means of ensuring the adequacy of our personal sorrow for our sins."[8] If we were to ask him how this is, he would seem to reply like this: "It is the hardest possible thing to be conscious of God's presence"; "we have no such consciousness of His presence as would make it possible for us to feel any part of that sorrow which we ought to feel"; but "the practice of Confession to another human being" produces "an entirely new reality to our confessions of sin, which was absent before."[9]

The argument is plain. We ought to be more penitent. We cannot deepen our penitence by secret confession to God because this is not real to us. So we resort to sacramental confession as a device to make it real. Mind you, some writers are candid enough to concede that the device does not by any means always work. Auricular confession is as prone to degenerate into a formality as any other confession, and Jack Winslow rightly says that it can be "an escape from honesty with our fellowmen. We can put off our mask before one who is pledged to secrecy, and put it on again amongst those with whom we live day by day"[10] and (he might have added) before God himself.

I fully agree that the danger of unreality in secret confession to God is great, but I submit that the remedy proposed is the wrong one. What is needed is not an artificial device to make God more real, but a resort to the biblical method. Have we forgotten the promises of Jesus about the Holy Spirit, that when he came in Pentecostal fullness he would convict of sin and glorify Christ, that is, reveal him and make him known (Jn 16:8, 13)? I rather doubt if faith in the confessional to bring deep conviction of sin in the presence of God can co-exist with a strong faith in the Holy Spirit. We need to recapture our belief that one of the God-appointed functions of the Holy Spirit is to make us know, feel, mourn, loathe, and forsake our sins; and if we are conscious of a superficial view of sin, our proper course of action is to cry to the Holy Spirit, not to flee to the confessional.

But how does the Holy Spirit bring conviction of sin? The instrument he uses is the Word of God. You may recall that the commination service has been mentioned several times in this book. It begins by bemoaning the prevalence of vice in those "dangerous days" and by desiring that public discipline will be restored to the church. Meanwhile, the remedy for the restraint of sin which it proposes is not confession but a "commination," that is a reading of "the general sentences of God's cursing against impenitent sinners" gathered from the Scriptures, "to the intent that . . . ye may the rather be moved to earnest and true repentance." The preaching of the law and the gospel can awaken and deepen penitence if the Holy Spirit confirms the Word. The result of Peter's sermon on the day of Pentecost was that the crowd were "cut to the heart" and cried out, "Brothers, what shall we do?" (Acts 2:37), while the same ministry of God's Word through the prophet Nathan brought repentance and confession to King David (2 Sm 12:1–13). If, therefore, we are conscious of a lack of conviction of sin in ourselves, or in the congregation we may have been called to serve, or in the church at large (as we undoubtedly must be today), the right course to pursue is to read the Word of God ourselves, and expound it faithfully to others, with a humble, earnest entreaty to the Holy Spirit to exercise his promised ministry and stir our sluggish consciences. The remedy is less precise, less concrete, less ready-made than the confessional, but I venture to say that it is more biblical and is therefore certain to be more effective.

Assurance of Forgiveness

The second benefit which auricular confession is said to bestow is an assurance of forgiveness. Let us agree with modern writers on this subject that deliverance from the bondage of guilt and a certainty of divine absolution were never more needed than they are in our twentieth century. Jack Winslow quotes the head of a large English mental home as having said: "I could dismiss half my patients tomorrow if they could be assured of forgiveness."[11] George MacLeod handles the subject with his customary force and eloquence. "It has been authoritatively claimed," he writes, "that some 60 per cent (of patients in Scottish mental hospitals) are suffering in some degree from a guilt complex," and he describes general practitioners who are "delayed in their work by the number of quite normal patients with an overflowing need to unburden their souls." "We live in a world," he goes on, "where literally thousands of our church members are in need of . . . release. . . . We live . . . in a vacuum where men simply are not freed."[12] He is not exaggerating. He is quite right. Men are crying out for forgiveness, and an assurance of it, for integration and release.

Once again we are agreed in the diagnosis, but disagreed about the cure. "I am concerned with the consequence of true confession," writes George MacLeod, "which is absolution." He describes what he calls the "fragrant and beautiful" system of penance which the early Celtic church introduced, with its "anam-chara" or "soul-friend," and urges a new synthesis of individual and corporate absolution.[13] Wilfred Knox tells us his problem quite candidly: "How can I be certain, so long as penitence is regarded simply as an attitude of the soul or a psychological state, that its depth and sincerity is sufficient to obtain forgiveness?" He later answers his own question: "The value of the Sacrament of Penance as a whole lies in the fact that it enables the penitent to express his sorrow for his sins by a formal outward action, and thereby satisfy himself that he has repented with a sufficient degree of sincerity to justify himself in believing that his penitence is acceptable to God." But the assurance comes not only from his own confession, but from the words of absolution by which "the penitent is assured of the fact that he has received that gift of forgiveness to an extent which justifies him in regarding his past sins as obliterated."[14] Other writers tell of their personal experiences of sacramental confession. "In that way, and that way alone, have we found peace," says Manasses, and adds: "indeed it is not perhaps too much to say that many have only in this way discovered the meaning of Christianity."[15] Jack Winslow is convinced that it could be "of rich blessing to many guilt-burdened souls."[16]

My purpose in quoting these passages is not to throw doubt on their sincerity or even their reality, but to ask again: Is this really the normal way which God has appointed, by which we sinners may find our burdens lifted, our guilt absolved, our sins forgiven, and peace? I think not. The Bible does not say it is. Nor does the Prayer Book. On the contrary, the way to receive assurance of forgiveness, like the way to receive conviction of sin, is through the Word of God as it is illumined to our hearts and minds by the Spirit of God. I certainly agree that there are psychological disorders, involving deep repressions and a guilt complex, which need medical treatment, rather than the ministry of God's Word. I fear there are also experiences of release through "getting something off one's chest" whether at confession or elsewhere, "making a clean breast of it" after "bottling it up" for years, which may be psychological rather than spiritual and may not give evidence of the actual forgiveness of God.

How can we receive God's forgiveness and be assured of it? Forgiveness is possible and available for sinners today, as we have seen, only because Jesus Christ bore our sins on the cross, enduring in our place their penalty and judgment. God accepts or "justifies" those who call upon Christ to save and cleanse them, and who trust him to do so. Forgiveness comes from what God has *done* in and through Christ; assurance comes from what God has *said* in and through Christ. He has promised to give rest to those who come to him and eternal life to those who trust in him (for example, Mt 11:28; Jn 6:37, 47). Can we not believe his promises? Remember not only what he has *done* and *said*, but what he *is*, eternal and unchangeable, true to his covenant, faithful to his Word. "God is not human, that he should lie, not a human being that he should change his mind. Does he speak and then not act? Does he promise and not fulfill?" (Nm 23:19). With this biblical way of assurance the Prayer Book is in full agreement. At Morning and Evening Prayer we pray for mercy and restoration "according to Thy promises declared unto mankind in Christ Jesus our Lord." In the absolution at Holy Communion the minister reminds us that God has "promised forgiveness of sins to all them that with hearty repentance and true faith turn unto Him," and immediately enforces this reminder by the four great gospel promises we call the comfortable words.

Yet his Word of promise is not the only means of assurance which God has given us. He knows that our faith is "brittle," to use Luther's word, and needs strengthening. Or, to change the metaphor, he knows how hard we find it to believe a "naked" word; so he has graciously "clothed" it for us to see, in the two sacraments of the gospel. Augustine called them *verba visibilia* (visible words), and Bishop Jewel added that "the substance of all sacraments is the Word of God."[17] They dramatize the promises of the gospel in such a way as to evoke and confirm our faith. Baptism, being unique and unrepeatable, is the sacrament of our once-for-all justification; Holy Communion, being repeatedly enjoyed, is the sacrament of our daily forgiveness. By them we are assured, audibly and visibly, of our acceptance and forgiveness. Once we have grasped this we can understand how mistaken medieval churchmen were to think of their sacrament of penance as "a second baptism"; how wrong Manasses is to write, "we were baptized and received remission of our sins but we have sinned since; we need a new baptism";[18] and how misleading it is for Eric James to say that confession "mediates 'Justification by Faith' in sacramental form."[19] We have baptism as our sacrament of justification and Holy Communion as our sacrament of forgiveness. Bishop Drury is right to say that "they both convey, in their several functions, the fullest possible promise of remission to those who truly repent. There is no place for any minor sacrament" to supplement them.[20]

God's way of assurance is, therefore, by his Word, proclaimed to us through the Scriptures and the sacraments, and apprehended by faith. One of the most urgent needs in the church of God today is a recovery of the simple biblical truth that the Christian life is a life of faith in response to God's Word. Faith feeds on the promises of God and grows healthy and strong by them. Why should we need the words of fallible men as a substitute for, or even supplement to, the infallible Word of God? A man, however experienced and perspicacious, cannot read our inner thoughts and motives. Only God knows our heart, and St. John makes this omniscience of God one of the means by which we may pacify our heart whenever it condemns us (1 Jn 3:19–20). Some may find it easier to believe the word of a visible man, but do we forget that God has called such to preach to us the message of forgiveness (Lk 24:47; Acts 13:38) and that he has graciously made his Word visible to us in the sacraments? Kenneth Ross writes: "If you would like to have heard Jesus say to *you*, 'Son, be of good cheer; thy sins be forgiven thee,' then you should make your confession." But no! Jesus speaks these words of comfort and assurance to my soul every time I come to him as a repentant, believing sinner, whether in response to the public preaching of his Word or in my private Bible reading or at the Lord's Supper. We need to meditate, in the eleventh chapter of the Epistle to the Hebrews, on the great heroes of faith in the Old Testament, to whom the Word of God came, who embraced it and staked their whole lives upon it, "being fully persuaded that God had power to do what he had promised" (Rom 4:21). It is God's will that we should become "mature in Christ" (Col 1:28), not continually resorting to men and depending on the words of men, but "fight the good fight of the faith" (1 Tm 6:12), hearing and receiving God's holy Word through Scripture and sacrament, laying fast hold of his promises, and refusing to let them go until "through faith and patience" we inherit them (Heb 6:12). This is the biblical way of assurance. It is the Church of England way too. Hooker summed it up in these words: "*We* (s.c. of the Church of England) labour to instruct men in such sort, that every soul which is wounded with sin may learn the way how to cure itself; *they* (s.c. of the Church of Rome), clean contrary, would make all sores seem incurable, unless the priest have a hand in them."[21]

But, it will be immediately objected, there are some people who simply cannot find peace that way. They try to lay down their burden at the foot of the cross but somehow cannot leave it there. Their conscience keeps stabbing them, nagging them, tormenting them; and however hard they try to pacify it by believing the promises of God, they fail. In such special cases confession "is not in reformed churches denied by the learneder sort of divines."[22] So wrote Richard Hooker, and added that its purpose was "for the strengthening of weak, timorous, and fearful minds." Similarly, in Ridley's words it is "to instruct, correct, comfort, and inform the weak, wounded, and ignorant conscience."[23] If men find their conscience "troubled with any weighty matter" (Visitation of the Sick), or, to use Tyndale's expressive word, "tangled,"[24] they should not hesitate to "repair to their learned curate or pastor, or to some other godly learned man, and show the trouble and doubt of their conscience to them, that they may receive at their hand the comfortable salve of God's Word."[25] It is for this that the Prayer Book makes provision, and we should avail ourselves of it in a time of special need. The reason why God's promises may not previously have brought peace to the soul is neatly expressed by Calvin: "It sometimes happens, that he who hears the general promises of God, which are addressed to the whole church, nevertheless remains in some suspense, and is still disquieted with doubts as to the forgiveness of his sins. But if he discloses secretly to his pastor his distress, and hears the pastor applying to him in particular the general doctrine, he will be straightly assured where formerly he was in doubt, and will be liberated from every trepidation, and find repose of conscience."[26]

This kind of resort to a minister is quite legitimate, and, of course, a minister should sympathetically welcome any person who comes to him with a troubled conscience, and should seek to quieten it by the particular application of the general promises of God. Nevertheless, it remains exceptional and should not be encouraged as a habitual practice. The Prayer Book is quite clear that the normal "way and means" to assurance and to preparation for Holy Communion is self-examination "by the rule of God's commandments," followed by confession of sin and trust in God's promises of mercy. It is only "if there be any of you, who by this means cannot quiet his own conscience" that he should come privately to his minister for "further comfort and counsel" (first exhortation). Not only should such an approach to the minister be exceptional, but, as Bullinger rightly commented, it should "rather be termed a consultation than a confession."[27] All notions of "sacramental confession," "judicial absolution," and "penance" are inappropriate to it. The minister is exercising a pastoral not a priestly function, in soothing a wounded conscience with the ointment of God's Word. If a visit of this kind is regarded as both pastoral and exceptional in character, no possible objection can be raised to it; it is one of every minister's sacred privileges. Bishop Ryle sums it up for us in writing: "Occasional private conference with a minister is one thing; habitual confession of sin, with habitual absolution, is quite another."[28] We might summarize the four changes made by the Reformers in this way: What had been an obligatory and habitual confession to a priest, involving the systematic enumeration of all remembered sins, became a voluntary and exceptional resort to a minister, to consult him about some special burden of conscience.[29]

Sanctification

The third argument which is adduced in favor of auricular confession concerns the penitent's growth in holiness or "sanctification." This is much insisted upon by Anglican writers. "One of the main purposes of the Sacrament of Penance," wrote Wilfred

Knox, "is to build up the character of the penitent by enabling him to gain grace to withstand temptation . . . the Sacrament is normally found to be of the utmost value in assisting the penitent in accomplishing this task."[30] It is for this reason that Eric James called his little book *The Double Cure*, taking the expression from Toplady's great hymn *Rock of Ages*:

> Be of sin the double cure,
> Cleanse me from its guilt and power.

Referring to the parable of the prodigal son again, he says that "if the cure isn't double, the prodigal will just 'pop home,' make his confession and be on his way back to the far country in no time."[31] It is because this aspect of auricular confession is regarded as so important that the person to whom, or in whose presence, the confession is made is commonly called not a "confessor" but a "spiritual director."

The two means by which his help is asked and given for sanctification are "penance" and "advice." The whole concept of penance is confused and unbiblical. It seems to have started with the Old Latin version of the Bible, which was followed by Jerome in the Vulgate. In these the Greek word for "repentance" (*metanoia*) was translated by *poenitentia*, and the verb *metanoein* by *poenitere* or *agere poenitentiam*. These inaccurate translations then crept into early English versions like Wycliffe's in the misleading expression to "do penance" instead of to "repent." We have seen how in the Middle Ages penance was regarded as a painful discipline or punishment to make satisfaction for sin. Still in the Roman Catholic Church today, although "the virtue of penance" means penitence, "works of penance" are "imposed on the penitent in atonement for the temporal punishment for sins which remain after the guilt of sin and its eternal punishment have been forgiven."[32] They are regarded as a "sacramental satisfaction" for sin. The Reformers repudiated these ideas as derogatory to Christ's perfect satisfaction for sin on the cross and replaced the words "penance" and "do penance" with "repentance" and "repent." It is sad that any notion of private "penance" should have been revived in the Church of England. Anglican writers who use it are careful to reject any suggestion that penance is a satisfaction for sin, but they do not speak in a united voice as to what it does mean. To Manasses it is "some small thing for you to do as a thank offering to God" or "as a sign of gratitude for the mercy of God's forgiveness."[33] To Wilfred Knox it is the penitent's express "recognition of the fact that the sins which he has confessed are actions for which he was morally responsible, and not merely the results of temperamental weaknesses which he had no power to control"; it is thus an acknowledgment of "his own guilt."[34] To Kenneth Ross it is "a token of the fact that you intend to turn over a new leaf." One is left wondering whether the "penance" is intended as a mark of guilt, gratitude, or resolution. The very uncertainty with which contemporary writers broach the subject, and the trivial nature of the "penances" imposed, would be good reasons for its final abandonment. In any case, the biblical way of giving evidence of repentance is the performance of good works of love and holiness (Mt 3:8, 10).

The second means of promoting the penitent's sanctification is advice. This is the "ghostly counsel and advice" referred to in the first exhortation at Holy Communion. There is nothing harmful here. One is only obliged to say that it is not strictly a part of "sacramental confession," since spiritual advice is given by all ministers to members of their congregation quite independently of the confessional. It can therefore hardly be advanced as an argument for the practice of habitual confession. It is rather an argument for a faithful pastoral ministry in the vestry and the study, in visiting the homes, and in meeting with small groups informally.

Although pastoral counselling should always be beneficial and not harmful, its chief peril seems to lie in the kind of situation envisaged by auricular confession, namely the regular interview of penitent with pastor. Whether it takes place in "confession" in church or in a consultation in the study, I do not think weekly or monthly visits to the minister are conducive to the person's spiritual health. We revert to our theme and assert that God's normal means for the edification of his people in his Word, "the word of his grace, which can build you up and give you an inheritance among all those who are sanctified" (Acts 20:32). There is a constant danger of clergy tying people to their apron strings, instead of encouraging them to develop a certain sturdy and healthy independence, as they rely more and more upon God himself. It is surely to this that Jesus referred when he warned us to call no man our "father," "Rabbi," or "instructor" on earth (Mt 23:8–12). We are to adopt towards no one in the church, nor require anyone to adopt towards us, the dependent attitude implied in the child-parent, pupil-teacher, servant-lord relationships. We are all brethren. We are to depend on God as our Father, Christ as our Lord, and the Holy Spirit as our Teacher. The ambition of every minister for his congregation should be so to warn every man and teach every man in all wisdom as to "present everyone" not dependent on his minister but "fully mature in Christ" (Col 1:28). Although occasional consultations can indeed do good, I cannot see that frequent visits to the parson, whether for "confession" or for "conference," are productive of true spiritual maturity.

The greatest single secret of spiritual development lies in personal, humble, believing, obedient response to the Word of God. It is as God speaks to us through his Word that his warnings can bring us to conviction of sin, his promises to assurance of forgiveness, and his commands to amendment of life. We live and grow by his Word.

We have sought in this chapter to examine impartially the claims advanced for the practice of auricular confession, from the point of view of the penitent's need. We have agreed that the need is there for a deeper repentance, assurance, and sanctification. But we have felt it right to insist that, according to the Scriptures, the remedy proposed is the wrong one. God's normal and natural way is not to send us to the confessional but to confront us with himself through his Word. It is commonly said, with regard to auricular confession in the Anglican Church, that "all may, none must, some should." Of these three assertions, I can only agree with the first: "all may," in exceptional circumstances. But I would replace the other two with "none should," since it is not God's ideal, though "some need." As Dean Goulburn correctly said about the provision made in the first exhortation, it is "not the best thing to be done, but the second best"; and this second best is like "walking on crutches."[35] I could not fail to be struck, when reading George MacLeod's pamphlet, to find that he employs the same metaphor. "The whole apparatus of confession and absolution," he admits with great candor, "is nothing more, and has never been anything more, than a crutch for the lame." He goes on to suggest that perhaps his reader is "an athlete in spiritual things," but ends: "for myself, I am lame."[36]

None of us walks perfectly uprightly. Varying degrees of spiritual paralysis disable us. But do not let us acquiesce in our lameness! We may feel the need of crutches from time to time. But let us look forward to the day when we can throw them away, when, like the cripple at the Beautiful Gate, through faith in the strong Name of Jesus Christ, our ankle bones receive strength, and leaping up we can stand and walk, and enter into the house of God, walking and leaping and praising God! (Acts 3:1–8).

Conclusion

The principle which we have sought to establish and illustrate in this book is that sin must be confessed only to the person or persons who have been offended and from whom forgiveness is therefore desired. Confession is never to a third party, both because he has not been offended, and because he is not in a position to forgive the sin. This is the simple reason why auricular confession is a practice to be deplored. It is not an answer to say that auricular confession is not "to a priest," but either to God through the priest or in the presence of the priest, or to the church represented by the priest. Such representative confession is neither recognized nor recommended in Scripture. If the sin has been committed against God, it should be confessed to God secretly; if it has been committed against the church, it should be confessed to the church publicly. Confessing such sins to a priest is not right, since it makes secret confession not secret through including another person and public confession not public through excluding the church.

This critical rejection of the practice of habitual auricular confession is not to be interpreted as due to a light view of sin or to a desire to make confession easier for the sinner. On the contrary, I believe we need to take the gravest possible view of sin, which the Bible does, as "this detestable thing" which God hates (Jer 44:4), which is responsible for the sin-bearing death of the world's Savior, the sorrows and sufferings of many people in this life, and the irretrievable ruin of others in the next. Our opposition to "sacramental" confession is to be attributed not to our low view of sin but to our high view of Christ and the perfection of his provision for the sinner's absolution. So let me, in conclusion, issue two practical appeals.

First, we need to *take the confession of sin more seriously*. "General Confession," writes Eric James, "may conceal a refusal to take sin seriously."[1] Yes, it may. But it need not, especially if it is no substitute for the conscientious confession of sin to God in secret.

Every biblical Christian must agree that one of the most evident symptoms of the church's contemporary sickness is our lack of a proper sense of the fact or the gravity of sin. It is an indication that the Holy Spirit, whose peculiar work it is to convict of sin, is being resisted, grieved, and quenched. Two of the strikingly vivid pictures of conviction of sin in the Bible are "weeping" and "blushing." Many men of God have wept over sin, not just over their own but over the sins of the church, the nation, and the world. Ezra wept over the disobedience of Jerusalem (Ezr 10:1), Jeremiah over their pride (Jer 13:17), Jesus Christ over their willful blindness (Lk 19:41–44). The psalmist could even write: "Streams of tears flow from my eyes, for your law is not obeyed" (Ps 119:136). If we should thus weep over the sins of others, how much more should we weep over our own, turning to the Lord with all our heart "with fasting and weeping and mourning" (Jl 2:12, see also Mt 5:4; 1 Cor 5:2; 2 Cor 7:2)? And if we should weep over our sins because we are sorry, we should also blush over them because we are ashamed (Ezr 9:6; Jer 6:15; 8:12).

This book is a plea for more confession, not less, but for better confession, and confession of the right kind. We need to be more disciplined in secret self-examination and detailed confession to God. This should be "habitual, thorough, compulsory."[2] We need to be more faithful and courageous in apologizing to those we have offended and in rebuking those who have offended against us. We need to press for a restoration in the

Anglican Communion, whatever the cost, of a seemly, biblical discipline in the local congregation when a public scandal has been caused.

My second appeal is that we should *take the forgiveness of sin more seriously also*. Christianity is a religion of forgiveness. God is willing to forgive sinners through Christ. We must forgive one another. The church has absolute authority to forgive and to restore to its fellowship those who have offended against it and been suspended, but have subsequently repented and confessed their sin. We need to demonstrate the forgiveness of God to a world burdened with guilt, and to a world torn by bitter animosities the way in which the disciples of Jesus are taught to forgive one another. We need more faith in the promises of God to rejoice in divine forgiveness; more love for each other to rejoice in human forgiveness. We need to exhibit before the world our Christian freedom—freedom from guilt and freedom from spite. We need to go on beyond forgiveness, and exploit the privileges which forgiveness makes possible, a great *parrhēsia*, boldness or outspokenness, both in our access to the throne of grace and in our fellowship with one another.

It is not by a revival of auricular confession, rightly discarded at the Reformation, that God wills these ends to be accomplished, but by humble submission to his Word, so that, confessing our sins and receiving his forgiveness, we may rejoice in the liberty with which Christ has made us free.

I cannot conclude better than with the words by which Dean Wace summed up the Fulham Conference: "Let the free forgiveness of the Gospel be boldly proclaimed, let men and women be persuaded, in reliance on it, to live a life of direct confession to God, direct reliance on Christ's absolution, direct communion with the Holy Spirit, and so we may best hope to maintain and develop that strong, frank, courageous, God-fearing, and God-trusting character which is the ideal of the English Church, and the glory of English Churchmanship."[3]

Conclusion

O Lord, we beseech Thee, mercifully hear our prayers, and spare all those who confess their sins unto Thee; that they, whose consciences by sin are accused, by Thy merciful pardon may be absolved, through Jesus Christ our Lord.

Commination Service

Some Official Anglican Statements

1. Convocation of Canterbury 1873 and 1877

On Friday, May 9th, 1873, the Upper House of the Convocation of Canterbury considered a petition which had been sent to them, signed by 483 priests. The penultimate request of this lengthy document was "that, in view of the widespread and increasing use of sacramental confession, your venerable House may consider the advisability of providing for the education, selection, and licensing of duly qualified confessors, in accordance with the provisions of canon law."

A full discussion took place, in which several bishops strongly asserted that the practice of habitual confession was "contrary entirely to the spirit of our Prayer Book" and indeed "entirely alien to the whole spirit of the Church of England." Archbishop A. C. Tait, who was in the chair, expressed his gladness that every bishop and member present "altogether repudiates the practice of habitual confession, and that they all state with the utmost distinctness that they consider the sacramental view of confession as a most serious error." A committee of the whole House was then appointed to consider the matter. On July 23rd of the same year it issued the "report on the teaching of the Church of England on the subject of Confession," which appears below. It was sent down to the Lower House on July 3rd, 1877, who on the following day resolved by sixty-two votes against six "that this House concurs in the Declaration on Confession sent down to it from the Upper House for consideration." The text is as follows:

> In the matter of Confession, the Church of England holds fast those principles which are set forth in Holy Scripture, which were professed by the Primitive Church, and which were reaffirmed at the English Reformation. The Church of England, in the Twenty-Fifth Article, affirms that penance is not to be counted for a sacrament of the Gospel; and, as judged by her formularies, knows no such words as "sacramental confession." Grounding her doctrines on Holy Scripture, she distinctly declares the full and entire forgiveness of sins, through the blood of Jesus Christ, to those who bewail their own sinfulness, confess themselves to Almighty God, with full purpose of amendment of life, and turn with true faith unto Him. It is the desire of the Church that by this way and means all her children should find peace. In this spirit the forms of Confession and Absolution are set forth in her public services. Yet, for the relief of troubled consciences, she has made special provision in two exceptional cases.
>
> (1) In the case of those who cannot quiet their own consciences previous to receiving the Holy Communion, but require further comfort or counsel, the minister is directed to say, "Let him come to me, or to some other discreet and learned minister of God's Word, and open his grief, that by the ministry of God's Holy Word he may receive the benefit of Absolution, together with ghostly counsel and advice." Nevertheless, it is to be noted that for such a case no form of Absolution has been prescribed in the Book of Common Prayer; and further, the Rubric in the first Prayer Book of 1549, which sanctions a particular form of Absolution, has been withdrawn from all subsequent editions of the said Book.
>
> (2) In the order for the Visitation of the Sick, it is directed that the sick man may be moved to make a special confession

of his sins if he feels his conscience troubled with any weighty matter, but in such case Absolution is only to be given when the sick man shall humbly and heartily desire it. The special provision, however, does not authorize the ministers of the Church to require from any who may repair to them, to open their grief in a particular or detailed examination of all their sins, or to require private confession as a condition previous to receiving the Holy Communion, or to enjoin or even encourage any practice of habitual confession to a priest, or to teach that such practice of habitual confession, or the being subject to what has been termed the direction of a priest, is a condition of attaining to the highest spiritual life.[1]

2. Lambeth Conference, 1878

At the second Lambeth Conference, which met in 1878, under the presidency of Archbishop A. C. Tait, the bishops considered a number of questions submitted to them and then issued an encyclical letter which summarized their conclusions. It took the form of five committee reports, and the fifth report included the following section E:

> Considering unhappy disputes on questions of ritual, whereby divers congregations in the Church of England and elsewhere have been seriously disquieted, your Committee desire to affirm the principle that no alteration from long-accustomed ritual should be made contrary to the admonition of the Bishop of the Diocese.
>
> Further, having in view certain novel practices and teachings on the subject of Confession, your Committee desire to affirm that in the matter of Confession the Churches of the Anglican Communion hold fast those principles which are set forth in the Holy Scriptures, which were professed by the Prim-

itive Church, and which were reaffirmed at the English Reformation; and it is their deliberate opinion that no minister of the Church is authorized to require from those who may resort to him to open their grief a particular or detailed enumeration of all their sins, or to require private confession previous to receiving the Holy Communion, or to enjoin or even encourage the practice of habitual confession to a priest, or to teach that such practice of habitual confession, or the being subject to what has been termed the direction of a priest, is a condition of attaining to the highest spiritual life. At the same time your Committee are not to be understood as desiring to limit in any way the provision made in the Book of Common Prayer for the relief of troubled consciences.[2]

3. Royal Commission on Ecclesiastical Discipline, 1906

The Royal Commission on Ecclesiastical Discipline was set up by King Edward VII on April 23rd, 1904 "to inquire into the alleged prevalence of breaches or neglect of the law relating to the conduct of Divine Service in the Church of England, and to the ornaments and fittings of churches."

It held 118 sittings, examined 164 witnesses, and reported on June 21st, 1906. Chapter V of the report is headed "Confession." After stating that the subject did not appear "to fall within the law relating to the conduct of Divine Service and to the ornaments and fittings of churches," the commissioners added that nevertheless they could not pass over in silence the evidence they had received that "the practice of habitual confession has increased" and that "it is pressed by some clergymen on their congregations as a duty, especially before Confirmation, and in some cases before receiving Holy Communion." The report continues:

It would seem to be impossible to reconcile such systematic arrangements as have been referred to with the practically unanimous declaration of 100 Bishops of the church set forth in the Encyclical Letter issued by the Lambeth Conference of 1878, that "no minister of the Church is authorized to require from those who may resort to him to open their grief, a particular or detailed enumeration of all their sins, or to require private confession previous to receiving the Holy Communion, or to enjoin, or even encourage, the practice of habitual confession to a priest, or to teach that such practice of habitual confession, or the being subject to what has been termed the direction of a priest, is a condition of attaining to the highest spiritual life."

The subject was not dealt with in the subsequent Lambeth Conferences (1888 and 1897); but we have no reason to doubt that in substance the declaration would be approved by the Episcopate of today, although the words "or even encourage" might, as was suggested in 1878 and subsequently, be thought by some to need modification for the purpose of meeting individual cases.

Note: Of the one hundred bishops present at the 1878 Lambeth Conference, only two dissented from the statement on Confession. They took exception to the words "or even encourage," but to nothing else. See Minute 13270 of the Evidence taken before the Royal Commission.

Bibliography

Allmen, J.-J. von, ed. *Vocabulary of the Bible*. London: Lutter-worth, 1958.

Becon, Thomas. "The Castle of Comfort." In *Early Works of Thomas Becon*. Vol. 2. Cambridge: University Press / Parker Society, 1844.

————. "The Potation for Lent." In *Early Works of Thomas Becon*. Vol. 1. Cambridge: University Press / Parker Society, 1843.

Bullinger, Heinrich. "Of Repentance and the Causes Thereof." The second sermon in *The Decades of Henry Bullinger*. Cambridge: Cambridge University Press, 1851.

Butterfield, P. D. *How to Make Your Confession: A Primer for Members of the Church of England*. London: SPCK, 1958.

Confession and Absolution. Report of a Conference held at Fulham Palace in 1901–2. Edited by Henry Wace. London: Longmans, Green, 1902.

Drury, Thomas W. *Confession and Absolution: The Teaching of the Church of England as Interpreted and Illustrated by the Writings of the Reformers of the Sixteenth Century*. London: Hodder and Stoughton, 1903.

Girdlestone, R. B., H. C. G. Moule, and T. W. Drury. *English Church Teaching on Faith, Life and Order*. London: C. Murry, 1898.

Goulburn, Edward Meyrick, Dean of Norwich. *Primitive Church Teaching on the Holy Communion*. New ed. London, 1912.

Hooker, Richard. *Of the Laws of Ecclesiastical Polity*. In *The Works of That Learned and Judicious Divine Mr. Richard Hooker*. 7th ed. Vol. 3, bk. 6. Edited by John Keble. Oxford: Clarendon, 1888.

James, Eric A. *The Double Cure: How to Receive Forgiveness*. London, 1957.

Jewel, John. *An Apology of the Church of England*. London: Cassell, 1888.

―――. *A Defence of the Apology of the Church of England*. Vol. 3. Cambridge: Cambridge University Press, 1848.

Homilies and Canons. London, 1914.

Knox, Wilfred L. *Penitence and Forgiveness*. London: SPCK, 1953.

Latimer, Hugh. *Sermons of Hugh Latimer*. London: Parker Society, 1844.

Lightfoot, J. B. *Commentary on the Epistle to the Philippians, 8th ed*. London: Cambridge University Press, 1885.

Litton, Edward. A. *Introduction to Dogmatic Theology: On the Basis of the Thirty-Nine Articles*. 3rd ed. London: R. Scott, 1912.

MacLeod, George F. *The Church of Scotland and the Confessional*. An Iona Community Pamphlet. London: SCM Press, 1958.

Manasses [pseud.]. *Go in Peace*. London: SPCK, 1958.

Meyrick, Frederick. *The Confessional*. London: Bemrose, 1905.

Ott, Ludwig. *Fundamentals of Catholic Dogma*. 5th ed. Cork: B. Herder, 1962.

Pollock, J. C. *Moody Without Sankey*. London: Hodder and Stoughton, 1963.

Ridley, Nicholas. *Letters of Bishop Ridley*. In *The Works of Nicholas Ridley, D.D., Sometime Lord Bishop of London, Martyr, 1555*. London: Parker Society, 1843.

Ryle, John. C. *Knots Untied: Being Plain Statements on Disputed Points of Religion, from the Standpoint of an Evangelical Churchman*. London: William Hunt, 1877.

Thomas, W. H. Griffith. *The Catholic Faith*. New impression. London: Longmans, Green, 1929.

Tyndale, William. *Expositions and Notes on Sundry Portions of the Holy Scriptures, together with The Practice of Prelates.* London: Parker Society, 1849.

———. *The Obedience of a Christian Man.* In *Doctrinal Treatises.* Cambridge: Cambridge University Press, 1848.

Warren, Max A. C. *Revival: An Enquiry.* London: SCM Press, 1954.

Wesley, John. *A Plain Account of the People Called Methodists.* In *Works of John Wesley.* 3rd ed. Vol. 8. London: John Mason, 1830.

Whyte, Alexander. *A Commentary on the Shorter Catechism.* Edinburgh, n.d.

Winslow, Jack C. *Confession and Absolution: A Short Guide for Today.* London: Hodder and Stoughton, 1960.

Notes

Notes to the Introduction

1. The Visitation of the Sick.

Notes to Chapter One

1. Examples of the "covering" of sin in an attempt to hide it are Jb 31:33; Ps 32:5; Prv 28:13, and of God's "covering" of sin in forgiveness Neh 4:5; Pss 32:1; 85:2.

2. Ps 103:12; Is 38:17; 44:22; Jer 31:34; Mi 7:19; Heb 8:12.

3. Heinrich Bullinger, "Of Repentance and the Causes Thereof," the second sermon in *The Decades of Henry Bullinger* (Cambridge: Cambridge University Press, 1851), 71.

4. See for example Mk 1:15; Acts 2:38, 44; 20:21; Heb 6:1.

5. For the confession of sin, see Lv 5:5; 16:21, 26, 40; Nm 5:7; Jo 7:19; Ezr 10:1; Neh 1:6; Ps 32:5; Prv 28:13; Dn 9:4, 20; Mt 3:6 = Mk 1:5; Acts 19:18; Jas 5:16; 1 Jn 1:9.

For the confession of faith, see Mt 10:32–33 = Lk 12:8–9; Jn 1:20; 9:22; 12:42; Rom 10:9; 2 Cor 9:13; Phil 2:11; 1 Tm 6:12; 1 Jn 2:23; 4:2; 2 Jn 7.

6. See for example Neh 9; Pss 32, 40, 51; 1 Jn 1:5–2:2.

7. Charles Biber, "Confess," in J.-J. von Allmen, *Vocabulary of the Bible* (London: Lutterworth), 1958.

8. Thomas Becon, "The Potation for Lent," in *Early Works of Thomas Becon*, vol. 1 (Cambridge: University Press / Parker Society, 1843), 100.

Notes to Chapter Two

1. William Tyndale, *The Obedience of a Christian Man,* in *Doctrinal Treatises* (Cambridge: Cambridge University Press, 1848), 266.

2. See also Is 59:1–9; Hos 6:6; Am 5:21–24; Mi 6:6–8.

3. Quoted in J. C. Pollock, *Moody Without Sankey* (London: Hodder and Stoughton, 1963), 234.

4. Pollock, *Moody Without Sankey*, 189.

5. See *Of Repentance* in the *Second Book of Homilies* (1562), 575.

6. Heinrich Bullinger, "Of Repentance and the Causes Thereof," the second sermon in *The Decades of Henry Bullinger* (Cambridge: Cambridge University Press, 1851), 85.

7. Richard Hooker, *Of the Laws of Ecclesiastical Polity*, in *The Works of That Learned and Judicious Divine Mr. Richard Hooker*, 7th ed., vol. 3, bk. 6, ed. John Keble (Oxford: Clarendon, 1888), iv, 2.

8. Hooker, *Ecclesiastical Polity*, iv, 3.

9. Hugh Latimer, *Sermons of Hugh Latimer*, vol. 1 (London: Parker Society, 1844), i, 426.

10. This phrase from Article XXXI (*Of the One Oblation of Christ Finished upon the Cross*) already occurred in the Forty-two Articles published in 1552.

11. Article XII, *Of Good Works*.

12. John Jewel, *A Defence of the Apology of the Church of England,* vol. 3 (Cambridge: Cambridge University Press, 1848), 352.

13. Tyndale, *Obedience of a Christian Man*, 267.

14. *Of Repentance*, 580.

Notes to Chapter Three

1. John Jewel, *A Defence of the Apology of the Church of England*, vol. 3 (Cambridge: Cambridge University Press, 1848), 351.

2. Alexander Whyte, *Commentary on the Shorter Catechism* (Edinburgh, n.d.), 191.

3. Bengt G. M. Sundkler, *Bantu Prophets in South Africa* (London: Lutterworth, 1948), quoted in Max A. C. Warren, *Revival: An Enquiry* (London: SCM Press, 1954), 69.

4. *Of Repentance* in the *Second Book of Homilies* (1562), 575.

5. John Wesley, *A Plain Account of the People Called Methodists*, in *Works of John Wesley*, 3rd ed., vol. 8 (London: John Mason, 1830), 258.

6. Wesley, *Plain Account,* 259.

7. Warren, *Revival,* 67–74, 118–21.

8. Charles Biber, "Confess," in J.-J. von Allmen, *Vocabulary of the Bible* (London: Lutterworth), 1958.

9. Definition of *homologeō* in the Grimm-Thayer Lexicon.

10. Edward A. Litton, *Introduction to Dogmatic Theology: On the Basis of the Thirty-nine Articles*, 3rd ed. (London: R. Scott, 1912), 357.

11. Jewel, *Defence of the Apology,* 354. See also 361.

12. Jewel, *Defence of the Apology,* 362.

13. In 2 Thes 3:14 the same Greek verb *sunanamignusthai* is used, but appar-

ently the man in question is not yet excommunicated, as he is still to be warned as a brother (v. 15).

14. Quoted in Thomas W. Drury, *Confession and Absolution: The Teaching of the Church of England as Interpreted and Illustrated by the Writings of the Reformers of the Sixteenth Century* (London: Hodder and Stoughton, 1903), 151.

15. Thirty-nine Articles of Religion of the Church of England (1563), 494.

16. A welcome new rubric is printed before the Holy Communion Service of the Canadian Prayer Book (1959), in which the minister is authorized to "refuse to administer the Communion" both to those "whom he knows to be living in grievous sin," if they will not repent, and to "those between whom he perceives malice and hatred to exist," if they obstinately refuse to be reconciled. The rubric adds that "before repelling any from the Lord's Table . . . the minister should consult with the Bishop or the Archdeacon," and that "after so repelling any, he shall within 14 days give a written account to the Bishop."

17. Jewel, *Defence of the Apology*, 356.

Notes to Chapter Four

1. John Jewel, *A Defence of the Apology of the Church of England,* vol. 3 (Cambridge: Cambridge University Press, 1848), 353.

2. Richard Hooker, *Of the Laws of Ecclesiastical Polity,* in *The Works of That Learned and Judicious Divine Mr. Richard Hooker,* 7th ed., vol. 3, bk. 6, ed. John Keble (Oxford: Clarendon, 1888), iv, 3, 6, 13.

3. *Homilies and Canons* (London, 1914), 577.

4. Frederick Meyrick, *The Confessional* (London: Bemrose, 1905), 22-23. Some of them are quoted in Hooker, *Ecclesiastical Polity*, iv, 16.

5. The statements that "private confession to God in prayer" and "confession to God before a priest" are equally legitimate alternatives, and that those who practice the one should not be offended by those who practice the other, have reappeared in the alternative South African Prayer Book (1954), in the third rubric before the *Form of Confession and Absolution*, and in the second rubric before the same form in the new Prayer Book of the Church of India, Pakistan, Burma and Ceylon (1960).

6. *Second Book of Homilies*, 577.

7. John C. Ryle, *Knots Untied: Being Plain Statements on Disputed Points of Religion, from the Standpoint of an Evangelical Churchman* (London: William Hunt, 1877), 271.

8. Quoted in Hooker, *Ecclesiastical Polity*, vi, 2.

9. Ludwig Ott, *Fundamentals of Catholic Dogma*, 5th ed. (Cork: B. Herder, 1962), 419.

10. Ott, *Fundamentals*, 417.

11. Ott, *Fundamentals*, 439.

12. Ott, *Fundamentals*, 418, quoting Jn 20:21, 23.

13. Ott, *Fundamentals*, 417.

14. Ott, *Fundamentals*, 422.

15. Ott, *Fundamentals*, 436.

16. Ott, *Fundamentals*, 423.

17. Ott, *Fundamentals*, 424.

18. Ott, *Fundamentals*, 424.

19. Ott, *Fundamentals*, 431.

20. *Confession and Absolution*. Report of a Conference held at Fulham Palace in 1901–2, ed. Henry Wace (London: Longmans, Green, 1902), 28.

21. *Confession and Absolution*, 70.

22. Manasses [pseud.], *Go in Peace* (London: SPCK, 1958), 84, 82, 86.

23. Wilfred L. Knox, *Penitence and Forgiveness* (London: SPCK, 1953), 79, 80.

24. Robert Barnes, *The Works of Dr. Barnes* (1573), 258.

25. Thomas Becon, "The Potation for Lent," in *Early Works of Thomas Becon*, vol. 1 (Cambridge: University Press / Parker Society, 1843), 566.

26. William Tyndale, *The Obedience of a Christian Man*, in *Doctrinal Treatises* (Cambridge: Cambridge University Press, 1848), 269.

27. John Jewel, *An Apology of the Church of England* (London: Cassell, 1888), 60.

28. Jewel, *Defence of the Apology*, 363.

29. See Prof. H. B. Swete's words at the Fulham Conference. *Confession and Absolution*, 15.

30. Letter to the clergy of Salisbury diocese, 1898, quoted by Thomas W. Drury, *Confession and Absolution: The Teaching of the Church of England as Interpreted and Illustrated by the Writings of the Reformers of the Sixteenth Century* (London: Hodder and Stoughton, 1903).

31. Hooker, *Ecclesiastical Polity*, vi, 8.

32. See J. B. Lightfoot's dissertation on "The Christian Ministry," appended to his *Commentary on the Epistle to the Philippians*, 8th ed. (London: Cambridge University Press, 1885) especially, 248–69.

33. William Tyndale: *Expositions and Notes on Sundry Portions of the Holy Scriptures, together with The Practice of Prelates* (London: Parker Society, 1848), 160.

34. Becon, "The Potation for Lent," 560.

35. Jewel, *Defence of the Apology*, 365.

36. Drury, *Confession and Absolution*, 248.

37. Drury, *Confession and Absolution*, 248–9.

38. In 1662 Convocation rejected the proposal to replace the word "minister" by "priest" as in the 1549 book.

39. R. B. Girdlestone, H. C. G. Moule, and T. W. Drury, *English Church Teaching on Faith, Life and Order* (London: C. Murry, 1898), 50.

40. In the 1928 Prayer Book a form of confession is supplied, and the rubric directs that the confession be made "in this or other like form."

41. It is significant that the American Prayer Book omits the form of absolution, adding instead in the rubric that "on evidence of his repentance, the Minister shall assure him of God's mercy and forgiveness."

42. Hugh Latimer, *Sermons of Hugh Latimer*, vol. 1 (London: Parker Society, 1844), i, 423.

43. Christopher Wordsworth quoted in Drury, *Confession and Absolution*, 179.

44. Ryle, *Knots Untied*, 258.

Notes to Chapter Five

1. Thomas W. Drury, *Confession and Absolution: The Teaching of the Church of England as Interpreted and Illustrated by the Writings of the Reformers of the Sixteenth Century* (London: Hodder and Stoughton, 1903), 137.

2. P. D. Butterfield, *How to Make Your Confession: A Primer for Members of the Church of England* (London: SPCK, 1958), 8.

3. Wilfred L. Knox, *Penitence and Forgiveness* (London: SPCK, 1953), 93.

4. Eric James, *The Double Cure: How to Receive Forgiveness* (London, 1957).

5. Butterfield, *How to Make Your Confession*, 9.

6. Manasses [pseud.], *Go in Peace* (London: SPCK, 1958), 54.

7. Eric James, *The Double Cure: How to Receive Forgiveness* (London, 1957), 8, 19, 39.

8. Knox, *Penitence and Forgiveness*, 13.

9. Knox, *Penitence and Forgiveness*, 51, 52.

10. Jack C. Winslow, *Confession and Absolution: A Short Guide for Today* (London: Hodder and Stoughton, 1960), 28–29.

11. Winslow, *Confession and Absolution*, 22.

12. George F. MacLeod, *The Church of Scotland and the Confessional*, an Iona Community Pamphlet (London: SCM Press, 1958), 3, 4, 5.

13. MacLeod, *The Church of Scotland and the Confessional*, 3, 7, 8.

14. Knox, *Penitence and Forgiveness*, 45, 46, 78, 79.

15. Manasses [pseud.], *Go in Peace*, 50, 57.

16. Winslow, *Confession and Absolution*, viii.

17. John Jewel, *A Defence of the Apology of the Church of England*, vol. 3 (Cambridge: Cambridge University Press, 1848), 353.

18. Manasses [pseud.], *Go in Peace*, 108.

19. James, *The Double Cure*, 10.

20. Drury, *Confession and Absolution*, 81–82.

21. Richard Hooker, *Of the Laws of Ecclesiastical Polity* in *The Works of That Learned and Judicious Divine Mr. Richard Hooker*, 7th ed., vol. 3, bk. 6, ed. John Keble (Oxford: Clarendon, 1888), vi, 2.

22. Hooker, *Ecclesiastical Polity*, iv, 154.

23. Nicholas Ridley, *Letters of Bishop Ridley*, in *The Works of Nicholas Ridley, D.D., Sometime Lord Bishop of London, Martyr, 1555* (London: Parker Society, 1843), 338.

24. William Tyndale: *Expositions and Notes on Sundry Portions of the Holy Scriptures, together with The Practice of Prelates* (London: Parker Society, 1848), 266.

25. *Of Repentance* in the *Second Book of Homilies* (1562), 577.

26. John Calvin, *Institutes*, III, iv, 14.

27. Heinrich Bullinger, "Of Repentance and the Causes Thereof," the second sermon in *The Decades of Henry Bullinger* (Cambridge: Cambridge University Press, 1851), 75.

28. John C. Ryle, *Knots Untied: Being Plain Statements on Disputed Points of Religion, from the Standpoint of an Evangelical Churchman* (London: William Hunt, 1877), 257.

29. A retrograde step has been taken in this matter by the Church of India, Pakistan, Burma, and Ceylon in their 1960 Prayer Book. Part III of this book is entitled "The Ministry of Reconciliation" and consists of an explanatory Preface, followed by two Forms for Public Use (a penitential service and a renewal of baptismal vows) and Forms for Private Use, namely, a form of confession to be used alone and "a form of confession and absolution in the presence of a priest."

The Preface opens with a welcome insistence on the necessity of repentance, confession to God, and reconciliation with our neighbor. However, after reference to general confession in church and personal confession in secret, the Preface proceeds to a description of "the Ministry of Reconciliation," a phrase which it applies to the gaining of an assurance of pardon either through the absolution pronounced in the public services or "through private absolution given to the individual penitent." It is immediately added that "the pastors of the Church are authorized and bound by the commission received in their ordination . . . to exercise this ministry when required."

This makes sad reading, for no mention is made of the public preaching of the Word of God, which is the normal means that God has appointed to bring forgiveness and assurance to the penitent believer. It is to this that St. Paul was referring when he first used the expression "the ministry of reconciliation." He meant not the pronouncement of a formal absolution, either public or private, but the proclamation of "the word of reconciliation" by the ambassadors of Christ (2 Cor 5:18–21). It is for this preaching ministry also, and not for private absolutions, that the priest is authorized by the words spoken at his ordination (as has been shown on page 59). Further, although there is a valuable provision in the Preface that the "fellow-Christian" whom a penitent consults may be either "an experienced and devout lay member of the church" or "his own or some other pastor," there seems to be a confusion as to what this resort to a fellow Christian is. It is said that "the individual is often helped to full confession by unburdening himself to a fellow-Christian." It is not clear from this whether the unburdening of oneself is regarded as itself a confession or as a help "to full confession." The distinction between an "unburdening" of oneself to friend or pastor (which should be occasional, not "often") and frequent or habitual "confession" is unhelpfully blurred. These things are different, and need to be clearly distinguished.

30. Knox, *Penitence and Forgiveness*, 91.

31. James, *The Double Cure*, 16.

32. Ludwig Ott, *Fundamentals of Catholic Dogma*, 5th ed. (Cork: B. Herder, 1962), 434, 435.

33. Manasses [pseud.], *Go in Peace*, 82, 91.

34. Knox, *Penitence and Forgiveness*, 63.

35. Edward Meyrick Goulburn, Dean of Norwich, *Primitive Church Teaching on the Holy Communion*, new ed. (London, 1912), 39, 54.

36. MacLeod, *The Church of Scotland and the Confessional*, 16.

Notes to the Conclusion

1. James, *The Double Cure*, 17.

2. W. H. Griffith Thomas, *The Catholic Faith,* new imp (London: Longmans, Green, 1929), 386.

3. *Confession and Absolution*. Report of a Conference held at Fulham Palace in 1901–2, ed. Henry Wace (London: Longmans, Green, 1902), 108.

Notes to the Appendix

1. *The Chronicle of the Convocation of Canterbury* (London, 1873), 558.

2. *The Six Lambeth Conferences 1867–1920* (London, 1920), 97.

Subject Index

Absolution, 22–23, 32–33, 58, 69–71; auricular confession and, 47, 48–53, 55–56, 75; Holy Communion and, 61, 72, 85; in Prayer Book, 3–4, 32–33, 58–64, 71–72, 85–86; by a priest, 47, 49–53, 55–56, 60, 75

Achan, 38

Adam and Eve, 6, 10, 49

Advice / council, 52, 60, 66, 76, 77–78, 85

Ananias and Sapphira, 38, 41–42

Anglican Communion, 58–59, 81–82; auricular confession, 46–48, 52–53, 67, 75–77, 79, 81–82, 86–87; Declaration on Confession, 85; general confession, 7–8, 15, 31–32, 46–47; Lambeth Conference, 1878, 86–87, 88; Morning and Evening Service / Prayer, 1, 4, 31–32, 61; repentance, 67, 77; Royal Commission on Ecclesiastical Discipline, 1906, 87–88; Thirty-Nine Articles of Religion of the Church of England (1563), 24, 40, 43, 47–48, 59, 85

Anglican Prayer Books: absolution, 3–4, 32–33, 58–64, 71–72, 85–86; Canadian Prayer Book, 94n16; Church of India, Pakistan, Burma, and Ceylon, 1960 Prayer Book, 94n5, 97n29; Communion, preparation, 3–4, 8, 31–32, 42–43, 48, 61, 75, 85–88; confession of sins, 3–4, 15, 31–32, 65–66, 74–75, 84; neighbors, relations with, 21, 24–25; ordination of priests / ministers, 59–60, 97n29; South African Prayer Book (1954), 94n5; Visitation of the Sick, 21, 24–25, 58–59, 61–63, 74, 85–86. *See also* Book of Common Prayer

Anglo-Catholics, 46–47, 52–53

Apologizing, 16, 19–20, 81

Apostles, 3, 40, 43; forgiving sins, 15, 50–51, 53–58

Attrition, 67

Augustine, 4, 44–45, 72

Auricular confession, to a priest, 46–48, 64, 67–68, 80–81; absolution and, 47, 48–49, 50–53, 55–56, 75; Anglican Communion, 3–4, 15, 31–32, 65–66, 74–75, 84; assurance of forgiveness, 69–71; Communion preparation, 47–48, 50–51, 60–61; priest and, 49–50; reciprocal, 21–22, 34–35; Reformers and,

14, 46, 47–48, 60–63, 65–66,
74–75, 82–83, 85–86; regular use
/ habitual, 34, 64–66, 77–78,
80–81, 84, 86–88; Roman Catholic, 50–53; sanctification, 75–76
Authority, 40; of church, 54–56;
judicial, 51, 53–54, 57–58, 62–63,
64, 75; transfer, by Jesus Christ,
54–57, 61–62, 63–64; Word of
God, 40, 53–54, 60–61, 62–63

Baptism, 34, 43, 52, 57, 72; sins
after, 47, 48, 50
Bellarmine, Cardinal, 50
Binding and loosing, 39–41,
44–45, 50, 53–55
Book of Common Prayer, 14, 24,
85, 87. *See also* Anglican Prayer
Books

Calvin, John, 74
Canadian Prayer Book, 94n16
Celtic church, 70
Chrysostom, John, 47, 54
Church, secular world and, 44
Church of England. *See* Anglican
Communion
Church of India, Pakistan, Burma,
and Ceylon, 1960 Prayer Book,
94n5, 97n29
Comfortable Words, four, 61, 72
Commination service, 22, 42,
68–69, 83
Communion, Holy, 17, 48, 87,
94n16; absolution and, 61, 72,
85; auricular confession and,
3–4, 8–9, 31–32, 77, 86–87;
preparation for, 31–32, 42–43,
48, 61, 75, 87–88
Compulsory confession, 23, 46, 53,
65, 81–82
Concealing / covering sins, 6–10,
11–12

Confession of Christ, 36–37
Conscience, 8–9, 16, 21, 48, 53,
60–61, 74–75, 85–86
Contrition, 66, 67–68, 70
Conviction of sin, 17, 22–23, 35–36,
67–69, 81; Word of God and,
71, 78
Corinth, 40–42, 45
Council of Trent, 50
Cranmer, Thomas, 16, 23–24,
47–48, 59

David, King, 11, 13–14, 69
Declaration on Confession, 85–86
Deterrent, 41–42
Disciplinary confession, 37–44
Discipline, church, 22–23, 24,
37–43, 53, 54–55; modern
church, 43–45, 81–82; rebuking,
vi–vii, 26–30, 41–42, 81–82

Edward VII, 87
Ephesus, 33–34
Eusebius, 54
Excommunication, 40–42, 44–45

Faith, 4, 14–15, 24, 68, 72–74, 79
Forgiveness, 3–5, 11, 14, 46, 61; assurance of, 61, 71–75; confession
and, 4–5; of neighbor, 16–17,
19, 24; power to forgive, 50–52,
53–54, 55–57, 63

General confession, 7–8, 15, 31–32,
46–47, 81
God, 18–19; relationship with,
6–8; secret confession to, 5,
6–7, 13–14, 15–17, 20–21, 47–48,
67–68
Gospel, the, 33, 53–54, 85; Comfortable Words, 61, 72; preaching, 3, 39, 50–51, 53–54, 57–58,
63–64, 69, 82

Gossip, 9, 27, 28
Great Commission, 55–56, 57
Guilt, 7–8, 25, 69–71, 77, 82; sins
   and, 2, 4–5, 14–15, 23, 37–38

Habitual confession, 34, 64–66,
   77–78, 80–81, 84, 86–88
Halifax, Lord, 52
Henry VIII, 42, 61
Hermann's German liturgy, 77
Holy Spirit, 35, 55–56, 61, 78, 82;
   conviction of sin, 17, 58, 68–69,
   81

Indulgences, 23
Innocent III, Pope, 46
Intolerance, 43–44

Jerome, 76
Jesus Christ, 10, 25–26, 40; confession and, 20–21, 28, 36–37, 64;
   forgiveness of sins, 3–5, 8, 14–15,
   17, 50–53, 56, 61–62, 71, 73; keys
   of kingdom / authority transfer,
   53–57, 61–62, 63–64; rebuking /
   discipline, 27–28, 29, 38–39, 41,
   44–45
John the Baptist, 26, 33–34, 64
Judgment, 7, 10, 38, 42, 71
Judicial authority, 51, 53–54, 57–58,
   62–63, 64, 75
Justice, 18–19
Justification, 18, 72

Keys of the kingdom of heaven,
   44–45, 63; authority transfer,
   50–52, 54–56; Reformers and,
   53–54. *See also* Binding and
   loosing
Kings Book of 1543, 48

Lambeth Conference, 1878, 86–87,
   88

Lateran Council of 1215, 23, 46
Latimer, Hugh, 23–24, 42–43, 48,
   62
Leo the Great, Pope, 42
Local church, 5, 39–40, 44–45,
   55
Lord's Supper / Table. *See* Com-
   munion, Holy
Luther, Martin, 32, 72

Methodism, 35–36
Middle Ages / medieval, 22–24,
   50, 59, 72, 76–77
Mishnah, 39
Moody, D. L., 19–20
Morning and Evening Service /
   Prayer, 1, 4, 31–32, 61
Moses, Law of, 25–26

Omission, sins of, 8–9, 32

Paul, apostle, 16, 33–34, 41–42,
   45, 54
Peace, 29–30, 70–71, 74
Penalty of sin, 22–23, 71
Penance, 22–24, 42, 66, 75
Penance, sacrament of, 65–66,
   67–68, 70, 72, 85; forgiveness
   and, 24, 42–43, 48, 50–51;
   history of, 22–23, 42; sanctifica-
   tion, 46, 75–77
Penitence, 8, 23–24, 50, 55, 67–69,
   70, 76
Persecution, 42
Peter, apostle, 40, 44–45, 54, 69
Prayer Book. *See* Anglican Prayer
   Books
Preaching, 33, 43, 59–60, 62, 73;
   gospel, 3, 39, 50–51, 53–54,
   57–58, 63–64, 69, 82
Priesthood, doctrine of, 50–53, 65
Primitive church, 22–23, 42, 47, 85
Private confession; to the of-

fended, 5, 18–22, 27–28, 34–35, 80–81; to a priest, 23–24. *See also* Auricular confession, to a priest
Prodigal son, parable of, 18, 67, 76
Public confession, 23, 33–37, 38–39, 42–45
Purgatory, 23
Puritans, 62

Rabbis / rabbinic, 39, 55, 78
Rebuking, vi–vii, 26–30, 41–42, 81–82
Reciprocal, auricular confession, 21–22, 34–35
Reconciliation, 21–22, 24–30, 34–35, 39, 57–58, 97n29
Reformation / Reformers: auricular confession, 14, 46, 47–48, 60–63, 65–66, 74–75, 82–83, 85–86; binding and loosing / keys of kingdom, 39, 53–56; discipline, church, 41–43; forgiveness of sins, 24–25, 48–49, 50–51, 53–54, 59–60, 65–66; penance, 22–24, 48, 76–77; Second Helvetic Confession, 63
Reformed Prayer Book, 48
Reform, of sinner, 41–42, 44
Remitting sins, 23–24, 39, 47, 51, 58
Repentance / forsaking sin, vi–vii, 12–17, 32–33, 54–56, 61–64, 67–69; church discipline and, 40–41, 42–43; neighbor, sins against, 28–29; penance and, 76–77
Restitution, 22–26
Restoration of fellowship / reconciliation, vii, 29–30, 35–36, 39–41, 82
Retaining sins, 39, 51–54, 56–57
Retribution, 41
Revival, 35–36

Roman Catholic Church: auricular confession, 46–47, 51–53; penance, 67–68, 76–77; priesthood, doctrine of, 50–53, 55, 65, 74
Royal Commission on Ecclesiastical Discipline, 1906, 87–88

Sacramental confession, 47–48, 77, 81; regular use of, 65, 67–68, 70–71, 75, 84–85; salvation and, 51–52
Sacrament of penance. *See* Penance, sacrament of
Salvation, 3, 14–15, 24–25, 50–54
Sanctification, 41–42, 46, 66, 75–79
Satisfaction, for sins, 23–24, 76–77
Savoy Conference, 62
Second Helvetic Confession, 79
Secret confession, to God, 5, 6–7, 13–14, 15–17, 20–21, 47–48, 67–68
Self-examination, 17, 75, 81
Sins, 3–5, 13–14, 81–82; concealing / covering, 6–10, 11–13; God, relationship with and, 6–8; guilt and, 2, 4–5, 14–15, 23, 37–38; moral hardening, 12–13; of omission, 8–9, 32; uncovering, 7–8, 9, 11–13, 17
Six Articles of 1539, 48
South African Prayer Book (1954), 94n5
South Africa, Zionist Church, 34
Specific confession, 16–17, 33–34
Spiritual health, 8–10, 78
Suffering, 2, 24, 80–81

Tait, Bishop A. C., 84, 86
Tertullian, 54
Testimonies, 35–36
Thirteen Articles of 1538, 47–48
Thirty-Nine Articles of Religion of

the Church of England (1563), 24, 40, 43, 47–48, 59, 85

Unbelievers, 7–8

Visitation of the Sick, 21, 24–25, 58–59, 61–63, 74, 85–86

Wace, Dean, 82
Word of God, 78; assurance of forgiveness, 61, 71–75; authority, 40, 53–54, 60–61, 62–63;

conviction of sin, 16, 48, 68–69, 71, 78–79; preaching, 43, 58–60, 62, 78; sanctification, 82, 85. *See also* Gospel, the
Wordsworth, Christopher, 62–63
Wordsworth, John, 55
Works, good, 24, 37, 77
Wurtemberg Confession, 33
Wycliffe, John, 76

Zacchaeus, 25–26
Zionist Church, South Africa, 34

Scripture Index

OLD TESTAMENT

Genesis
3:7-10   6

Leviticus
5:5   92
6:4-5   25
16:21   92
16:26   92
16:40   92

Numbers
5:5-7   25
5:7   92
23:19   71
35:30   38

Deuteronomy
19:15   38

Joshua
7:19   38, 92

2 Samuel
12:1-13   69

Ezra
9:6   81
10:1   81, 92

Nehemiah
1:6   92
4:5   92
9   92

Job
31:33   92

Psalms
18:16   36
32   11-12, 92
32:1   22, 92
32:3-5   8
32:5   26, 92
34:6   36
40   92
40:2-3   36
51   13, 92
51:4   14
51:17   67
85:2   92
90:8   5
97:10   13
103:12   92
116:3-8   36
119:136   81
139:1-4   20

Proverbs
9:7   27

9:8   27
10:12   9
10:17   27
11:13   9
12:1   27
13:1   27
15:10   27
15:15   27
15:31   27
15:32   27
17:9   9
19:25   27
27:5   27
28:13   6, 15, 27, 92
28:23   27
29:1   27

Isaiah
1:13-17   19
38:17   92
44:22   92
53:6   32
59:1-9   92

Jeremiah
6:15   81
8:12   81
13:17   81
31:34   3, 92
44:4   80

Scripture Index

Daniel			23:8–12	78		20:21		92
9:4	92		23:13	54		20:21–23		52
9:20	92		26:28	3		20:23	51, 52, 53, 55,	
							57, 60, 62, 92	
Hosea			Mark			20:24		56
6:6	92		1:4	33				
10:8	10		1:5	33, 92		Acts		
			1:15	92		2:37		69
Joel			2:5	50		2:38	3, 54, 57, 92	
2:12	81		2:7	56		2:44		92
			2:17	56		3:1–8		79
Amos			2:19	56		3:19	3, 57	
5:21–24	92		2:28	56		5:1–11		38
			11:25	29		8:14–16		54
Micah						10–11		54
6:6–8	92		Luke			13:38		73
7:19	92		3:3	33		13:38–39	3, 57, 63	
			3:8	33		15:7		54
			3:10–14	33		19:18		92
NEW TESTAMENT			3:19	26		19:18–19		33
			7:29	57		20:21		92
Matthew			7:47	50		20:32		78
3:6	33, 92		11:52	54		22:16		57
3:8	77		12:2–3	10		24:16		16
3:10	77		12:8–9	92		26:17–18		57
5:4	81		15:18	18		26:18		40
5:9	30		15:21	18				
5:23–24	21, 34		17:3–4	28–29		Romans		
5:28	20		19:1–10	25		3:19		2
6:12–15	29		19:41–44	81		3:20		17
7:1–5	28		24:33	56		4:21		73
10:32–33	92		24:46–49	57		10:9		92
11:28	71		24:47	3, 57, 63, 73		12:18		30
16	53							
16:19	40, 53, 55		John			1 Corinthians		
18	53, 55		1:20	92		5		45
18:5	27		6:37	71		5:1		40
18:15	28		6:47	71		5:2	40, 81	
18:15–17	38, 41		9:22	92		5:5	41, 54	
18:17	39		12:42	92		5:9–11		41
18:17–18	45, 55		16:8	68		5:12–13	41, 44	
18:18	39, 40, 53		16:13	68		5:13		40
18:22	29		20	53		11:28		17

11:30	41	1:28	73, 78	**James**			
11:31	17, 44	3:15	29	5:14	21		
14:26	37			5:16	21, 34, 92		
		1 Thessalonians		5:19–20	28		
2 Corinthians		1:5	58	5:20	9		
2	41						
2:5–11	40	**2 Thessalonians**		**1 Peter**			
2:6	41	3:14	41, 93	2:24	3		
5:18–21	58, 97			3:11	30		
5:21	3	**1 Timothy**		4:8	9		
7:2	81	1:20	40, 41	4:17	44		
7:10	67	2:5	64				
9:13	92	5:20	26, 42	**1 John**			
		6:12	73, 92	1:5–2:2	92		
Galatians				1:7	16		
6:1	28	**2 Timothy**		1:8–9	4		
6:2	37	4:2	26	1:9	16, 92		
				2:1–2	64		
Ephesians		**Titus**		2:23	92		
1:7	3, 57–58	1:13	26	3:4	2		
4:15	35	2:14	44	3:19–20	73		
5:11	26	2:15	26	4:2	92		
5:12	49	3:10	41				
5:25–27	44	3:10–11	41	**2 John**			
				7	92		
Philippians		**Hebrews**					
2:11	92	6:1	92	**Jude**			
		6:12	73	23	49		
Colossians		8:12	92				
1:13	40	10:24–25	37	**Revelation**			
1:14	58			6:16–17	10		

 Langham
PARTNERSHIP

Langham Partnership is a global fellowship working in pursuit of the vision God entrusted to its founder John Stott—

to facilitate the growth of the church in maturity and Christ-likeness through raising the standards of biblical preaching and teaching.

Our vision is to see churches in the majority world equipped for mission and growing to maturity in Christ through the ministry of pastors and leaders who believe, teach and live by the Word of God.

Our mission is to strengthen the ministry of the Word of God through:
- nurturing national movements for biblical preaching
- fostering the creation and distribution of evangelical literature
- enhancing evangelical theological education

especially in countries where churches are under-resourced.

Our ministry

Langham Preaching partners with national leaders to nurture indigenous biblical preaching movements for pastors and lay preachers all around the world. With the support of a team of trainers from many countries, a multi-level programme of seminars provides practical training, and is followed by a programme for training local facilitators. Local preachers' groups and national andregional networks ensure continuity and ongoing development, seeking to build vigorous movements committed to Bible exposition.

Langham Literature provides majority world preachers, scholars and seminary libraries with evangelical books and electronic resources through publishing and distribution, grants and discounts. The programme also fosters the creation of indigenous evangelical books in many languages, through writer's grants, strengthening local evangelical publishing houses, and investment in major regional literature projects, such as one volume Bible commentaries like *The Africa Bible Commentary* and *The South Asia Bible Commentary*.

Langham Scholars provides financial support for evangelical doctoral students from the majority world so that, when they return home, they may train pastors and other Christian leaders with sound, biblical and theological teaching. This programme equips those who equip others. Langham Scholars also works in partnership with majority world seminaries in strengthening evangelical theological education. A growing number of Langham Scholars study in high quality doctoral programmes in the majority world itself. As well as teaching the next generation of pastors, graduated Langham Scholars exercise significant influence through their writing and leadership.

To learn more about Langham Partnership and the work we do visit **langham.org**